STUDIES IN COMMUNICATION

VOLUME **2**

Communication Theory and Interpersonal Interaction:
Selected Proceedings From the Fourth
International Conference On Culture
and Communication

COMMUNICATION AND INFORMATION SCIENCE

A series of monographs, treatises, and texts
Edited by
MELVIN J. VOIGT
University of California, San Diego

William C. Adams • Television Coverage of the Middle East
William C. Adams • Television Coverage of International Affairs
William C. Adams • Television Coverage of the 1980 Presidential Campaign
Alan Baughcum and Gerald Faulhaber • Telecommunications Access and Public Policy
Mary B. Cassata and Thomas Skill • Life on Daytime Television
Hewitt D. Crane • The New Social Marketplace
Rhonda J. Crane • The Politics of International Standards
Herbert S. Dordick, Helen G. Bradley, and Burt Nanus • The Emerging Network Marketplace
Glen Fisher • American Communication in a Global Society
Oscar H. Gandy, Jr. • Beyond Agenda Setting
Oscar H. Gandy, Jr., Paul Espinosa, and Janusz A. Ordover • Proceedings from the Tenth
    Annual Telecommunications Policy Research Conference
Edmund Glenn • Man and Mankind: Conflict and Communication Between Cultures
Gerald Goldhaber, Harry S. Dennis III, Gary M. Richetto, and Osmo A. Wiio • Information
    Strategies
Bradley S. Greenberg • Life on Television: Content Analyses of U.S. TV Drama
Bradley S. Greenberg, Michael Burgoon, Judee K. Burgoon, and Felipe Korzenny • Mexican
    Americans and the Mass Media
Cees J. Hamelink • Finance and Information: A Study of Converging Interests
Robert Landau, James H. Bair, and Jean H. Siegman • Emerging Office Systems
John S. Lawrence and Bernard M. Timberg • Fair Use and Free Inquiry
Robert G. Meadow • Politics as Communication
William H. Melody, Liora R. Salter, and Paul Heyer • Culture, Communication, and
    Dependency
Vincent Mosco • Broadcasting in the United States
Vincent Mosco • Pushbutton Fantasies
Kaarle Nordenstreng • The Mass Media Declaration of UNESCO
Kaarle Nordenstreng and Herbert Schiller • National Sovereignty and International
    Communication
Ithiel de Sola Pool • Forecasting the Telephone
Dan Schiller • Telematics and Government
Herbert I. Schiller • Who Knows: Information in the Age of the Fortune 500
Indu B. Singh • Telecommunications in the Year 2000
Jennifer Daryl Slack • Communication Technologies and Society
Dallas W. Smythe • Dependency Road
Sari Thomas • Studies in Communication Volumes 1–2
Janet Wasko • Movies and Money

In Preparation:

Heather Hudson • Telecommunications and Development
James Larson • Television's Window on the World
Kenneth Kraemer and William Dutton • Modeling as Negotiating
Armand Mattelart and Hector Schmucler • Communication and Information Technologies
Vincent Mosco • Proceedings from the Eleventh Annual Telecommunications Policy Research
    Conference
Everett Rogers and Francis Balle • The Media Revolution in America and in Western Europe
Herbert I. Schiller • Information and the Crisis Economy
Keith R. Stamm • Newspaper Use and Community Ties
Sari Thomas • Culture and Communication
Tran Van Dinh • Independence, Liberation, Revolution
Barry Truax • Acoustic Communication
Georgette Wang and Wimal Dissanayake • Continuity and Change in Communication Systems

STUDIES IN COMMUNICATION

VOLUME **2**

Communication Theory and Interpersonal Interaction:
Selected Proceedings From the Fourth
International Conference On Culture and
Communication, Temple University, 1981

Edited by

SARI THOMAS
Temple University

 ABLEX Publishing Corporation
Norwood, New Jersey 07648

Library of Congress Cataloging in Publication Data

International Conference on Culture and Communication
    (4th : 1981 : Temple University)
    Communication theory and interpersonal interaction.

(Studies in communication ; v. 2)
    Bibliography: p.
    Includes index.
    1. Intercultural communication—Congresses. 2. Interpersonal
communication—Congresses. 3. Communication—Congresses. 4. Ideology—
Congresses. 5. Culture—Congresses. I. Thomas, Sari, 1949-   . II. Title.
III. Series: Studies in communication (Norwood, N.J.) ; v.2.
HM258.I573   1981   302.2   83-25650
ISBN 0-89394-134-8

ABLEX Publishing Corporation
355 Chestnut Street
Norwood, New Jersey 07648

Contents

Introduction

SARI THOMAS

The Conference on Culture and Communication is a multi-disciplinary meeting which endeavors to explore the commonality of many fields from a communication perspective. The Conference schedules daily paper presentations and symposia on Communication Theory; Research Methodology and Philosophy of Social Science; Interpersonal Interaction; Government, Industry, and Culture; Communication and Ideology; Mass Media and Acculturation; Art as Cultural Artifact; and Education and Communicational Competence; and offers special evening lectures.

*   *   *

> . . . communication might be considered, in the broadest sense, as the active aspect of cultural structure. (Birdwhistell, 1970, p. 251)

The Conference at which papers in these volumes were delivered is designed to present scholarly efforts that, when taken together, reflect study of the basic interactive paradigm as suggested above by Birdwhistell. This model, in brief, proposes that the social universe may be examined from two interrelated perspectives; first, exteriorly, as *culture*, and second, interiorly, as *communication*. In this sense, culture may be seen as the *structure* of human organization at any given point in time or space, and as comprising (1) material conditions, (2) standardized actions (e.g., medical practices, agricultural techniques), and (3) worldviews and values. Clearly, none of these aspects of culture is a static phenomenon, and, even when they appear to be stable and unchanged over time, a considerable amount of energy must be expended (although not necessarily consciously) to maintain that order. The *system* that is and produces that energy (for maintenance *or* change) may be understood as *communication*.

This theoretical model does not stray far afield from more classic understandings of both "culture" and "communication". In certain schools of anthropology, for example, culture is generally thought of as ". . . the component of accumulated resources, immaterial as well as material, which the people inherit, employ, transmute, add to, and transmit." (Firth, 1951, p. 27) In the field of communication, the phenomenon of communication is ordinarily understood as that process by which information is transmitted. Thus, the earlier-presented model serves not to redefine these concepts, but rather to integrate them. In other words, it is possible to see the history of humankind as being both a record-keeper of its artifacts, practices, and beliefs and, at the same time, a changing process of interaction. While acknowledging that human beings are capable of having a past which produces the present and is always forwarded to the future, we simultaneously may analytically separate (1) the organization of any one 'moment' in the past or present (culture) from (2) the process which brought forth the moment and delivers it to the future (communication). However, it should be clear that while, for purposes of analysis, one may separate the two phenomena, in practice, their lives are inextricably bound in dialectic fashion. By the very force of its presence, the structure must inevitably affect the system.

All the papers in these volumes, in one way or another, are attempts to arrive at an understanding of some portion of this order and/or process. However, as the papers were competitively selected from those presented at a multi-disciplinary, open-format conference, they are not intended to represent evenly all areas germaine to the study of social structure and system. Instead, there were two major emphases in the selection process: first, that a paper include interesting theory and/or data not typically available in standard social-science texts, and, second, that there be represented a good deal of highly contemporary culture and communication issues.

*   *   *

Although much attention in the area of communication study is directed to mass-media practices and effects, it should not be inferred that work in this area is limited to such issues. This volume, in fact, includes recent work concerned with general theoretical issues of human communication systems as well as more specific analyses of the nature and processes of interpersonal relations.

The first section, Communication Across Cultures, presents papers detailing various aspects of information transmission as they are differentially effected by distinct cultural orders. In the second division, Communication Interaction, analyses of specific types of interpersonal processes *within* a given culture are offered.

The third section, Communication and Ideology, is concerned with the transmission process whereby information is culturally integrated to achieve various sociopolitical programs. Method in Culture Study, the section which follows, provides a special focus on academic ideology and its ramifications on those conceptual bodies and programs designed for the exploration of human social order and behavior.

The last section, Communication and Education, includes papers detailing how learning in the context of formal instruction may be influenced by those cultural perspectives and practices assumed.

REFERENCES

BIRDWHISTELL, R. L. (1970). *"Kinesics and Context: Essays on Body Motion Communication."* Philadelphia: University of Pennsylvania Press.

FIRTH, R. W. (1951). *"Elements of Social Organization."* London: Watts.

PART I

COMMUNICATION
ACROSS CULTURES

1

Some Cross-Cultural Studies of the Reciprocal Causal Relation between Communication and Culture

**W. BARNETT PEARCE, MARSHA HOUSTON STANBACK,
and KYUNG-WHA KANG**
University of Massachusetts
Amherst, Massachusetts 01002

The mobility and interdependence of the contemporary world and the consequent inevitability of intercultural contact have created considerable academic interest in intercultural interaction. The flurry of current research in this field has tended to generate two types of literature. First, ethnographic and quasi-ethnographic descriptions have provided accounts of communication behavior in various cultures and of the problems likely to arise when people of various cultures meet. These studies have done much to alert us to the influence of culture on communication processes. Second, theoretical and research reports have described factors differentiating successful from unsuccessful intercultural communication. For example, some theorists suggest a set of communicative skills or strategies (e.g., "empathy" or "tolerance for ambiguity") to describe or measure the competence of intercultural interactants; and others present meticulously categorized skills which comprise the "how-to-do-it" in various cultures (e.g., how to present a gift in Korea). These approaches have proved useful tools for intercultural educators and trainers.

Despite their obvious practical utility, neither current ethnography nor current theory has gone very far toward accomplishing what we feel should be the goal of communication research: to illumine the relationship between culture and the communication process. In our struggles toward this objective, we have concluded that any effort at theory building about human beings must transcend the *content* of specific cultures and yet be sensitive to the vast array of possible cultural *contexts*. This means that, in order to account for cultural variation, communication theories must be constructed at a higher level of abstraction than those currently represented in the literature. Operating within a specific cultural milieu, researchers are unable to distinguish between regularities that are inherent to human interaction in general and regularities that are a result of their own worldview. The theories generated by such an approach are cultural theories of communication, bound by their content—their epistemological orientation—to a specific culture. We are arguing for a *trans*cultural theory which can subsume all cultural variations in human communication. An important test of such a theory is its power to explain the "real world" phenomena of everyday communicative interaction within and across a variety of cultures.

Some recent scholarly developments provide a transcultural vantage point for the researcher (see Pearce and Cronen, 1980). One outcome is the development of communication "action theory." "Action theory" enables the theorist to see the common processes that occur in different cultural contexts. The *content* of those processes may be culture-specific, but their *structure* is comparable across cultures.

This paper demonstrates how action theory is reflected in our conceptualization of communication, summarizes the major tenets of action theory, and illustrates how we have used them in our efforts to understand the diversities of culture and communication through intracultural, cross-cultural, and intercultural analyses.

PRINCIPLES OF ACTION THEORY

Every cultural group has its own "logic" by which members make sense out of their daily experiences. The logic of a culture is imbedded in the meaning structures of individual members and is reflected in their attitudes and behavior. The content of those logics are the basis for the formation of a cultural worldview which functions as a common window to the world for members of that culture, mandating how a "brute fact" is to be transformed into an "institutional fact." The content of these institutional facts reveal differences between cultural groups.

Like any other object of human perception, conscious or unconscious, the activity of communicating is filtered through different worldviews. The result is the existence of vastly different ideas about the nature of human communication in different times and/or places (Pearce and Kang, 1980, pp. 2-4). Participation in communication has different significance for members of different cultural backgrounds.

Action theory purports to identify a common process in different cultural contexts which allows us to interpret cultural differences in terms of the relationship between culture and communication. We suggest that it is a theory of communication and culture, abstract enough to be content-free on the one hand as well as to be context-sensitive on the other, so that it is a viable way of accounting for the "real" experiences of individuals in their own social circumstances. The following is a summary of the basic principles of action theory presented in an escalating fashion, with each point building upon its previous one.

First, human actions are creative. Persons have the power to move, touch, and affect things, and in doing so create the environments which they and others interpret and respond to (Pearce and Kang, 1980, p. 11). Social realities are human creations. Our conception of humankind is of active, purposeful creators of meaning instead of as passive reactors in the stimulus-response chain. Even the most mundane forms of daily activities of human beings, e.g., casual chit-chat, are seen as having creative effects. Social reality is considered in terms of its meaning to the individual. Human experience is not of raw sensory data but of interpretations according to existing meaning structures. Social reality does not consist of "things in themselves," e.g., "the thing that breaks your toes when you kick it," but of "things as named."

Up to this point we have used the term "culture" interchangeably with "social reality" or "context." Obviously we take a semiotic conceptualization of culture (Geertz, 1973). We regard culture in terms of how it resides in the meaning system of its members. Culture is the result of "human conspiracy" (Calder, 1976, p. 10) to learn and to train others to act and to interpret actions properly. By definition, persons from different cultures act and interpret actions differently, thus rendering communication across cultures fundamentally problematic. This conceptualization of culture cuts across the various units of cultural analysis, from the smallest unit of individual persons to the larger ones of national or regional cultures. Therefore, all communication is "intercultural" to some extent. This feature of communication requries communication scholars/researchers to reorient themselves away from the traditional monocultural framework to a multicultural one.

The idea that human actions create reality has occurred to many people but usually has not been expressed very boldly. Among the earliest and clearest contributors to the emergence of the idea were Weber, Malinowski, and Austin. Weber (1968) emphasized the role of "ideas" as causal forces in history. He argued that it is the subjective orientation to action of individual actors which should be the subject matter of sociological inquiry. This brought a new "interpretive" trend in the field of Western sociological inquiry, exemplified in the present ethnomethodological works of Garfinkel (1967) and others. These interpretive sociologists in the Weberian tradition believe that the task of social science lies not in the use of specific behavior as exemplifications of general concepts, e.g., "social class," but in reducing these concepts to understandable action, i.e., to the actions of participating individuals.

Thus the subject of study in this newly-founded interpretive social science became the social reality as created by persons as it caused them to act in particular ways.

Consistent with the idea that human action is creative, is the notion of communication as action instead of as a vehicle of expressing thought. The idea was first introduced by Malinowski (1923) in his ethnographic studies of the South Pacific islanders. He began his studies with the traditional Western assumption that language pictures reality and that communication is reflected thought based upon a conceptualization of an isomorphism between reality, thought, and language. However, during the course of his investigations, Malinowski discovered that communication did not work this way. Brilliantly interpreting his data, he concluded that persons use language for several purposes, such as phatic communion, coordination of tasks, rituals, and magic and that language must be evaluated in terms of the functions which it serves rather than as a description of thought or reality. This notion of communication as action was extended by speech act theorists such as Austin (1962), who demonstrated that there are many language uses, some of which should be considered as *performatives* to be evaluated in terms of *"felicity conditions"* rather than *"truth conditions."*

Second, the social realities created by individuals are not necessarily orderly. In fact, they are usually disorderly (Watzlawick, 1976). If one's worldview included the assertion that there is an Ultimate Reality "out there" uninfluenced by human agency, constituted through some divine creation or natural law, one could assume an underlying pattern which gives order beneath the variations in appearances. However, if such an order exists, it is comfortably *below* the array of variously disordered social realities in which persons live. Considering the fact that individuals are reflexive beings whose actions do not merely reflect the context in which they occur but also have the power to change the context or create new ones, it should be expected that the actions of groups will produce confused, contradictory, and, sometimes, paradoxical realities. A theory of human action, communication included, must be able to account for this disorder.

The idea of the disorderly nature of social realities should discomfort traditional Western scholars, whose epistemology is based upon the existence of a "pattern which connects." To the extent that discomfort occurs, it reveals the ethnocentricity of traditional Western science. However, the fact of disorder does not imply an inability to do research or theory, but it does change the nature of the researcher's function. Rather than trying to find the "laws" which govern a category of phenomena, the researcher/theorist becomes a model-builder, describing the type, degree, and consequences of order and disorder. Their work is valuable to the extent that they approximate the interpreted/created reality of actors, and not the Ultimate

Reality. To the extent that a theorist's work provides insight into the creative process and leads to heuristic questions, it is useful.

Third, as a radical extension of the idea of inherent disorderliness of human creation, action theory proposes that there is a reciprocal, causal relationship between human actions and social reality; human actions reflect the context in which they occur but also, in return, influence those contexts. And if one should consider all social behavior as having some communicative value, our final statement is that the reciprocal, causal relationship between human actions and social realities should be investigated primarily in terms of communication.

However, this reciprocal, causal, or morphogenic relationship between culture and communication is conceptually and methodologically difficult. It is difficult to think or write clearly in English about reciprocal, causal relationships because the grammar is linear. Also, most Western research methods are designed to test linear causality or correlation between events.

The major problem with this theory, however, is its poor fit with conventional wisdom about what a theory should look like. About the turn of the century, Bertrand Russell proposed a solution to the problem of paradoxical reflexivity that had plagued Western thought since Zeno. His "theory of logical types" noted that some statements function both to describe a class and as a member of the class described. The solution: "Don't do that." Following Russell, theorists have endeavored to keep class-inclusive and class-included statements separate.

Action theory is a Russellian nightmare. The content of the theory explicitly describes itself. It violates Russell's theory of types, but there is now reason to believe that it is valid (see Pearce and Cronen, 1980.) Action theory leads to two lines of research, one which treats it as a description of a class and one which treats it as a member of that class.

People in every culture communicate and think about communication. While there are some differences between the communication *behavior* characteristic of various cultures, there are greater differences in the way they *think about* communication. An analysis of various cultures produces an array of "cultural theories of communication," each of which can be subsumed under the theory of a reciprocal causal relationship. Research following from this principle identifies a coherence between the cultural theories of communication and the way communication occurs within each culture. These studies provide evidence for—but certainly not "proof of"—the reciprocal causal relationship.

Two of our research projects attempted to establish coherence between communication and culture as an indication of a reciprocal, causal relationship. The first study is a cross-cultural analysis of "reticence" as a communicative behavior (Kang and Pearce, 1980). The paper argues that cultures guide individual communicative acts in terms of whether reticence or self-assertion is prized, and these communication acts create social contexts which reinforce the social institutions and ways of thinking which shape communicative acts, and so on.

Western societies, in an ideal sense, place a high value upon discovery of truth and knowledge. Combined with a trust in human ability to arrive at this truth if one were to think correctly and logically, they regard reticence as a pathological communication act or a failure of the individual to participate in the discovery of truth. Therefore, the normative communication behavior becomes one of self-assertiveness. In short, the culture has guided the kinds of communication behavior that are carried out in society. On the other hand, self-assertive communication behavior leads to the creation of certain social institutions, which would not have happened if reticence were a highly valued behavior, e.g., self-assertiveness training programs, the sanctification of the freedom of speech, freedom of press, and family patterns in which children are as much initiators of change as parents. In other words, communication has guided culture.

Compare this with a traditional East Asian society in which Confucianism has been the dominating cultural force for centuries. The prime value in these cultures lies in *morality* rather than in *truth*. The individual is a mere element in an undifferentiated world the ideal state of which is one of "harmony." One can achieve this harmony if one tries *not* to distinguish him/herself by remaining unassertive of the individual self. In such cultures, reticence is regarded as a manifestation of moral cultivation instead of as a pathology. No wonder that the idea of the "free market place of ideas" did not originate in these cultures, and even when imported from the Western societies, as it has been during the recent past, it does not carry the sacredness that it does in the West.

The second study selected Afro-American culture as a place to investigate the reciprocal, causal relationship. Analysis of Black American communication often focuses on linguistic or rhetorical phenomena without making the important link between Black talk and the Black worldview. Stanback (1980) emphasized the reciprocity between previously identified Black communication phenomena and the Black American cultural "logic" in an analysis of Richard Pryor's monologues. She argues that Pryor's phenomenal popularity among Blacks can be attributed, at least partially, to his accurate representation of communicative forms recognizable to all Blacks, but most often used by working class men like the characters Pryor portrays. Pryor's monologues function much as Smitherman (1977, p. 73) contends everyday conversation among working class Black men functions: intertwined with talk about personal experiences such as drinking, encounters with the police, or women won and lost, are "lessons and precepts about life and survival."

Such personal narratives are the phenomena out of which shared definitions of reality are created in an oral culture such as Black America.

The second line of research treats action theory as a member of a class. It assumes that those who believe the principles of action theory themselves comprise a culture, and if action theory as a class inclusive term is true, then the members of the culture who believe action theory will communicate in ways which are shaped by and give shape to that theory. At the least, this suggests that those who accept action theory must develop new repertoires of communication skills; it may also imply a radically new set of social institutions. How do people who accept action theory communicate? Some do research about communication and culture which differs in some important ways from tradition. The existence of this research program itself counts as evidence which supports the validity of action theory.

CONCLUSION

Action theory provides a perspective which transcends the *content* of particular cultures while remaining sensitive to the array of cultural *contexts* in which communication occurs. The move made by the theory is to describe a reciprocal causal relationship in which particular cultural values/beliefs/ institutions and particular communication phenomena are "special cases." The basic claim is that *whatever* cultural window persons use to interpret the world affects their actions, and *whatever* actions they perform affects their culture.

This claim is at a higher level of abstraction than the cultural theories of communication which have emerged during human history. It is also curiously reflexive, because the theory itself comprises a culture as we have defined it, and the acts of analyzing situations, doing research, etc., tend to create a culture consistent with those acts. This reflexivity places the theory and research consistent with it in a special class.

The kind of studies we have done have, at best, established a coherence between communication and culture, they do not produce "proof" of the reciprocal morphogenic relationship of the type sought by most researchers in the Anglo-American tradition. However, that type of "proof" may well not be available—or desirable. We do not believe that a theory is a set of rigorously defined statements which describe reality. Rather, we see theory as an invitation to look at the world in a particular way; as a metaphor or art-object which shapes the thought and vision of the observer more than representing objective reality.

The ultimate test of this theory is whether it *works* in the way that it *describes* culture and communication as working. If the theory works, it will create a culture of persons whose actions (including their selection of research projects) are shaped by their theory, and the theory will be in-formed by the actions they perform. Hopefully, that culture will be aware of its own morphogenic forces, able to incorporate without denial or trivialization the content of other cultures, and sensitive to the array of contexts which exist within and between cultures.

REFERENCES

AUSTIN, J. L. (1962). "How to Do Things with Words." New York: Oxford University Press.

CALDER, N. (1976). "The Human Conspiracy." New York: Viking.

GARFINKEL, H. (1967). "Studies in Ethnomethodology." Englewood Cliffs, NJ: Prentice-Hall.

GEERTZ, C. (1973). "The Interpretation of Cultures." New York: Basic Books.

KANG, K.-W., and PEARCE, W.B. (1980). "Reticence: A Transcultural Analysis. "(Paper presented to the Speech Communication Association, New York City.)

MALINOWSKI, B. (1923). The problems of meaning in primitive languages. In O. K. Ogden and I. A. Richares (Eds.), "The Meaning of Meaning," pp. 296-336. New York: Harcourt and Brace.

PEARCE, W. B. and CRONEN, V. (1980). "Communication, Action, and Meaning: The Creation of Social Realities." New York: Praeger.

PEARCE, W. B., and KANG, K.-W. (1980). "Action Theory: Some Implications of a New Development in Western Thought for Communication Theorists and Practitioners." (Paper presented to "Communication Theory from Eastern and Western Perspectives". East-West Communication Institute, East-Wester Center, Honolulu, Hawaii.)

SMITHERMAN, G. (1977). "Talkin and Testifyin: The Language of Black America." Boston, MA: Houghton Mifflin.

STANBACK, M. H. (1980). "Features of Black Language and Communication in Richard Pryor's Monologues." (Paper presented to the Speech Communication Association, New York City.)

WATZLAWICK, P. (1976). "How Real is Real?" New York: Random House.

WEBER, M. (1968). "Economy and Society, An Outline of Interpretive Sociology." G. Roth and C. Wittlich, (Eds.). New York: Bedminster.

2

Reflexivity in Cultural Systems of Meaning

JOHN W. LANNAMANN
University of Massachusetts
Amherst, Massachusetts 01002

The validity of any distinction between modern and traditional cultures is fundamentally related to the validity of comparing cultures per se. While the heterogeneity of cultures is commonly accepted, theorists differ on whether structural similarity or content-based difference is the appropriate unit of analysis for cross-cultural studies. An early representation of the content-based approach is found in Tylor's 1871 definition of culture. He indicates that culture is an aggregate "which includes knowledge, belief, art, morals, law, custom and any other capabilities and habits acquired by man as a member of society" (Tylor, 1929, p.1). From this perspective, the generality of cross-cultural comparison is limited by the researcher's ability to collate the sociological details of two or more cultures. In contrast to Tylor's position, Levi-Strauss's (1963) acknowledgement that we must analyze each society "in order to discover, behind the chaos of rules and customs, a single structural scheme existing in different spacial and temporal contexts" indicates that cross-cultural comparisons are useful if a sufficiently abstract and molar unit of analysis is employed.

The purpose of this paper is to suggest a structurally based dimension for the comparison of various cultures. Specifically, this paper examines the role of reflexive interpretive procedures in cultural systems of meaning. Several theoretical perspectives are relevant to the study of reflexivity in systems of social meaning. The following sections explore the theories of Weber, Schutz, and Garfinkel, and the psychological theory of George Kelly.

WEBER'S INTERPRETIVE SOCIOLOGY

The interpretive sociology of Weber provides a utile foundation for the investigation of structural variations among cultures. Weber avoids the pitfalls of listing culture specific details by positing typical actions (Weber, 1947). To Weber, these theoretically conceived pure types are the appropriate subject matter for sociological investigation. Weber classifies four types of social action according to modes of orientation. Traditionally oriented action inextricably tied to historical pattern is seen as a distinct type of social action. Weber suggests that individuals whose actions are oriented by tradition perceive that the means employed for achieving a historically defined end are sacred. A second type of orientation to action is based on the affects and states of feeling of the actor. Weber terms this type of orientation affectual. Orientation of action in terms of absolute value forms the third component of Weber's analytic schema. Actions motivated by absolute value tend to be self-conscious acts directed toward fulfilling individual convictions. This orientation to action differs from the traditional orientation in that the means employed in accomplishing a specific end are variable and consistently planned for by the actor. A fourth type of social action identified by Weber concerns actions oriented by expedient rationality (*zweckrational*). Weber (1947, p. 117) states that "action is rationally oriented to a system of discrete individual ends . . . when the end, the means, and the secondary results are all rationally taken into account and weighed."

The use of Weber's schema of pure types of social action makes it possible to perform cross cultural comparisons. He cautions the reader against attempting to describe a social action in terms of only one or another of the four orientations to action. Weber (1947, p. 117) argues that his classification of the modes of orientation provides a typology "to which actual action is more or less closely approximated." Yet this disclaimer does not negate the utility of the pure-types analysis. Cultures may be described by the common commitments of individuals to a subjective orientation to action. From this perspective, culture is the product of shared subjective orientations to action rather than the domain specific content of action.

THE PHENOMENOLOGIST POSITION OF SCHUTZ

Schutz is also interested in the subjective meaning of action. Like Weber, he focuses on typifications of motivations to act, but unlike Weber, he argues that these typifications must be the constructs of the individual and not those of the observer. Schutz (1964-1971, Vol. 1, p. 354) points out that Weber's ideal types of action represent an imposed construct by the social scientist and, therefore, do not belong to the "common-sense thinking of man within everyday life." The realization of an individual's typifications requires a phenomenological approach to the study of social action. Schutz (1964-1971, Vol. 1, p. 11) states that the "simplest complex of meaning in terms of which an action is interpreted by the actor is its motives." He distinguishes actions motivated by purposes (the "in order to" motive) from actions motivated by reasons or causes (the "because of" motive). Schutz (1964-1971, Vol. 2, p. 13) goes on to say that "social things are only understandable if they can be reduced to human activities, and human activities are only made understandable by showing their in-order-to or because motives."

Schutz points out that typifications emerge in the actor's everyday experience of the world. Although he argues that the subjective experience of individuals gives rise to a knowledge of typical actions, Schutz (1964-1971, Vol. 1, p. 348) recognizes that the greater portion of an individual's knowledge is "socially derived, handed down to him by his parents and teachers as his social heritage." Yet it is impossible for an outsider to understand a given social setting without a knowledge of the typical social roles, typical expectations of behavior, and the typical motives of a situated activity. Thus, from a phenomenological standpoint, cross-cultural comparison is difficult. Schutz (1964-1971, Vol. 1, p. 348) claims that the "whole system of types under which any social group experiences itself has to be learned by a process of acculturation."

Weber's work has been criticized by Schutz because it imposes the social scientist's constructs upon the subjective experience of the individual. Schutz's formulations are weakened by precisely the opposite problem. He suggests that the constructs used for the analysis of social action must be the actor's own typifications, and that these typifications must be learned through a process of acculturation. Yet a social scientist endeavoring to understand the experience of a social group can become acquainted with the group's typifications only in terms of the researcher's typifications brought to the setting. Rausch claims that there is no such thing as a zero order history of a relationship (Rausch et al., 1974). Bateson's (1972) discussion of deutero-learning, the ability to learn how to learn, supports this claim. The natural result of phenomenological investigations is a recursive spiral of typifications, and the researcher seeking the goal of true intersubjectivity will sense the frustration of the tortoise in Zeno's paradox.

THE ETHNOMETHODOLOGICAL PERSPECTIVE

The ethnomethodological perspective of Garfinkel shares Schutz's emphasis on the practices of common-sense knowledge concerning social structures. Garfinkel (1967, p. vii) writes that ethnomethodological studies analyze "everyday activities as members' methods for making those same activities visibly-rational-and-reportable-for-all-practical-purposes, i.e., 'accountable,' as organizations of commonplace everyday activities." Central to the ethnomethodological endeavor is the concept of indexicality. Platt (1980) states that indexicality refers to the accomplishment of meaning in context. Like

Schutz's phenomenology, Garfinkel's work stresses the context-dependent accomplishment of meaning. Garfinkel claims that the concept of a context-in-general is meaningless and is, in fact, itself indexical. The appropriate subject matter for an ethnomethodologist is the way in which members bring indexical expressions to closure. Thus, ethnomethodology is directed toward understanding the situated practices of members involved in the production of meaning.

Understanding how individuals produce meaning necessitates an understanding of how they rationally account for their activities. Platt (1980, p. 23) suggests that individuals do this by justifying "whatever meaningful content they have produced through reference to cultural and social rules and by reference to familiar conceptions of the ways in which the world is socially ordered." Rational accounting is a method used by members for the retroactive justification of activities. By appealing to cultural rules, actors produce meanings for activities.

Although the ethnomethodological position cannot address contexts in general, it does provide a useful model for the analysis of meaning production *in* various cultures. The production of meaning structures through rational accounting transcends context. Garfinkel implies that rational accounting is an activity inseparable from the production of meaning. The extent to which this claim is correct is the extent to which rational accounting is a useful concept for cross-cultural analyses.

On the surface, Garfinkel's approach avoids the Escher-like nature of the intersubjectivity problem found in Schutz's work. Garfinkel investigates the *practices* members use to accomplish meaning. Platt (1980) points out that ethnomethodology is concerned with the ways in which the actors make sense of completed activities. To an ethnomethodologist, there is no social order divorced from the methods used by actors in unique situations. However, the researcher who attempts to understand the derivation of the "social order" upon which actors justify their completed activities (i.e., rational accounting) is again faced either with a recursive spiral of meanings due to the ethnomethodological ambivalence concerning the etiology of the "social order," or the questionable assumption that members are empty headed performance containers constantly creating anew the social world.

PERSONAL CONSTRUCT THEORY

The psychological perspective of George Kelly (1963) brings closure to several incomplete formulations appearing in both the interpretive and the interpretive/phenomenological perspectives. His work provides an escape route from the interpretive sociologist's external construct dilemma and the phenomenologist's recursive spiral of meanings.

Kelly adopts the model of "Man as Scientist" for the study of personality and suggests that it is the psychiatrist's duty to recognize a person's *own* constructs. He points out that each individual constructs his/her *own* constructs, and thus, constructs the world in terms of perceptual patterns used to anticipate future events. These patterns or "personal constructs" for making sense out of the world are based on the recognition of both similarities and differences among cues. The notion of typifications found in the work of Schutz resembles Kelly's notion of personal constucts only in that they are models of experience based on similarity. However, Kelly emphasizes that a construct is only meaningful if it contains both similarity and contrast. Kelly states that an individual assigns meaning to events, persons, and phenomena by recognizing both what a thing is *and* what it is not. This conceptual move is crucial to Kelly's theory because it puts a lid on the phenomenologist's problem of the spiral of meaning. Schutz's typifications are binary representations based on similarities identified by members. To say that a given characteristic is not typical of an object is merely to exclude if from the domain of the typification. From this perspecitve, a midget is just as not tall as a fire alarm. The implication of this binary characteristic of typifictions is that the researcher must make successive approximations of a member's typifications. Kelly's approach avoids this inelegance by recognizing that individuals create meaning by simultaneously defining what a thing is *and* what it is not. Thus, to know that someone perceives another as being "strong" is not enough. An understanding of how that person organizes meaning requires that the researcher become familiar with the person's definition of the contrast to the notion of "strong." The terms "strong" and "weak" denote a different perceptual pattern than that denoted by "strong" and "gentle" or "strong" and "kind." Therefore, Kelly postulates that individuals anticipate persons and events by employing a system of dichotomous constructs.

The application of Kelly's model to the study of culture is instructive. Kelly (1963, p. 94) indicates that it is the similarity of construal processes that defines a culture. He writes that "People belong to the same cultural group not merely because they behave alike, nor because they expect the same things of others, but especially because they construe their experience in the same way." This position takes into account the subjective experience of individuals, emphasizing the process of constructing social reality. It provides a foundation for a theory of social action which is not tied to the material base of a culture. Rather, a Kellian model of culture is based upon the similarity of individual's expectations of each other, similarities resting on common constructions of the social experience.

The various formulations of Weber, Schutz, Garfinkel, and Kelly provide the theorist with a set of powerful tools for cross-cultural analysis. Grafting one theorist's ideas onto those of another need not be seen as metatheoretically inconsistent. Each theorist acknowledges the necessity of dealing with the subjectivity of social action.

The perspective taken in this paper is informed by Weber's conception of subjective orientations to action, Schutz' and Garfinkel's conception of the practical accomplishment of meaning in situated activities, and Kelly's conception of dichotomous personal constructions as perceptual filters for the interpretation of social experience. Specifically, culture may be described as a social system characterized by a common type of orientation toward action from which members accomplish meaning through their situated practices and through the interpretation of action according to construed expectations.

REFLEXIVITY IN SYSTEMS OF SOCIAL MEANING

A common theme appearing in the writings of Weber, Schutz, Garfinkel, and Kelly is the influence of action on the alteration and redefinition of social context. In Weber's work, this influence is hinted at in his discussion of expedient rationality. Reflexivity is implied in Schutz and Garfinkel's discussions concerning retroactive meaning construction and in Kelly's treatment of the experientially based construct change.

It is helpful to couch these various notions of reflexivity in a unifying and rigorous description of reflexivity. Hofstadter (1979, p. 10) provides such a description. He writes that reflexivity exists when "by moving upwards (or downwards) through the levels of some hierarchical system, we unexpectedly find ourselves right back where we started."

The concept of hierarchical organization is central to an understanding of reflexivity. Pearce and Cronen (1980, p. 130) suggest that individuals organize meaning hierarchically. They write that "a theory of persons as processors of information must describe several levels of meaning and the organization within and among levels." The following levels are suggested as constituting a hierarchical model representative of the contexts within which individuals orient and interpret symbolic acts.

Level I. *Content* level meanings include the denotative function of nonverbal and verbal messages.

Level II. *Speech acts* refer to the relational level meanings which define the relationship between interactants. Messages are recognized as communicative events or acts and are best understood as performing functions rather than referencing objects or events. The interpretation of the message "You are a prompt person" is most informative when one recognizes that the message performs the speech act "Compliment" as well as simply declaring the alacrity of the person.

Level III.   *Episodes* are "communicative routines which communicators view as distant wholes, separate from other types of discourse, charcterized by special rules of speech and nonverbal behavior and often distinguished by clearly recognizable opening or closing sequences" (Gumperz, 1972). As a frame or context for patterned sequences of speech acts, episodes form the fields in which the rules governing speech acts exist.

Level V.   *Relationships* are individuals' definitions of the bonds between themselves and others.

Level VI.   *Life Scripts* are the broad patterns of relationships and episodes which comprise a person's self-image and expectations of future communicative events.

Level VII.   *Cultural Patterns* represent the archetypal patterns (constructs) in which individuals organize episodes, relationships and life-scripts. These patterns are structured by systems of logic which define cultural groups.

In Weber's analysis, ends may serve as the context for evaluating means. He suggests that persons whose actions are oriented by expedient rationality can alter either component of the means/end relationship. The rational negotiation of the end toward which actions are directed must also redefine the means used to reach the end. When means provide the possibility of redefining the end which previously served as context, reflexivity exists. An example of a reflexive loop in this analysis would be the case where the adolescent, who had previously spent time interacting with others in order to be a "street-wise" tough guy, began to realize that his interactions with others could be interpreted in two ways. Either his interactions with others required him to be a follower, in which case he could never be a real tough guy, or his interactions demonstrated that he was so tough that he no longer needed to interact with others in order to confirm his membership in the culture of tough guys. In either case the means for reaching the end seem to alter the original end.

Schutz (1964-1971, Vol. 2, p. 11) refers to similar phenomenon. He writes that "When an action is completed, its original meaning as given in the project will be modified in the light of what has actually been carried out, and it is then open to an indefinite number of reflections which can ascribe meaning to it in the present tense." Here again actions redefine context. This form of retroactive analysis of meaning is given a central position in Garfinkel's work. He refers to this characteristic of meaning production as reflexivity. Platt (1980, p. 13) suggests that when ethnomethodologists refer to reflexivity they are referring to "the members' continuous review, assessment, interpretation and reinterpretation in the flow of situated activities." Thus, from an ethnomethodological perspective, reflexivity is essential to the accomplishment of meaning.

Kelly's theory of personal constructs also provides for the influence of actions on social context. Kelly posits that individuals are continuously adapting their constructs in a way which will provide them with the greatest predictive power. This trial and error redefinition of constructs is based upon the individual's experience. Constructs generated in social actions become the pattern for perceiving the action.

A demonstration of reflexivity is provided by Hinkel's extension of Kelly's work. Hinkel (1965) found that changes in higher levels of a person's system of constructs have a substantial impact on subordinate constructs. For example, if one employs the concept "friendship" to the message, "Your backhand needs work," the meaning for the message is entirely different from the meaning which would emerge if the concept of "domination" was employed. Hinkle also found that changes in the lower levels of meaning influence change at the higher levels. This concept of change is a reflexive one. If tennis partners generally construe comments about weak spots in terms of friendship, an occasional disagreeable comment will not alter the higher level construal of friendship. If, however, one partner continues to make disagreeable comments, it is likely that the high level construal of friendship will be altered.

For heuristic purposes, two kinds of hierarchical influence may be postulated. Contexts which serve as guides for the ongoing production of meaning may be said to exert "contextual" influence. In the first example above, the message, "Your backhand needs work," is made meaningful by referencing the appropriate context. Here the notion of friendship influences the production of the meaning for the message. This is an example of contextual influence. In the second example, the lower level meanings (continuous disagreeable comments) imply that the context must be redefined. This form of upward influence of acts on context may be termed "implicative" influence (Cronen et al., 1980).

It is interesting to note that the concepts of contextual and implicative influence are indistinguishable in the ethnomethodological tradition. There are several reasons for this, the most important of which is the ethnomethodologist's conception of the person. The person, from their perspective, is the set of exhibited activities—nothing more or less. Unlike Kelly's constructivist position, the ethnomethodologists postulate no meaning structure separate from the situated activities of members. Platt (1980, p. 41) argues that "Ethnomethodological theory assumes that what people carry in their heads is not enough to accomplish the experience of coordinate action." The implicative influence of acts in contexts is therefore the only realizable method of accomplishing meaning.

Reflexivity, when viewed as a variable ratio of contextual and implicative influences on social action, is an important component of a meaning based, structural analysis of culture and cultural change. Implicative influence, the influence of action on the alteration and redefinition of social context is central to the definitions of culture in the interpretive, ethnomethodological, and constructivist traditions. It is intriguing to consider how various cultures differ in the extent to which social actors can alter hierarchical social contexts through their actions. In other words, to what extent are contexts inflexible and insulated from change? The dual concepts of implicative and contextual influence provide useful measures of how much reflexivity is present in cultural systems of meaning. In a traditional culture, we would expect that reflexive change is limited since to be traditional means to embrace the historically determined patterns of meaning and action (Lerner, 1958). In such a system, contextual influence is greater than implicative influence. In contrast, modern cultures may be characterized as reflexive systems of meaning because they exhibit a more equal mix of contextual and implicative influences.

REFERENCES

BATESON, G. (1972). The logical categories of learning an communication. *In* G. Bateson (Ed.), "Steps to an Ecology of Mind." New York: Ballantine.

CRONEN, V.E., JOHNSON, K.M. and LANNAMANN, J. (1980). "Paradoxes, Double-Binds, and Reflexive Loops: A Comparison of Two Theoretical Perspectives and a Suggested Methodology." (Paper presented to the Theory and Methodology Workshop of the National Council on Family Relations Annual Convention, Portland.)

GARFINKEL, H. (1967). "Studies in Ethnomethodology." Englewood Cliffs, NJ: Prentice Hall.

GUMPERZ, J.J. (1972). "Directions in Sociolinguistics." New York: Holt.

HINKLE, D.N. (1965). "The Change of Personal Contructs from the Viewpoint of a Theory of Construct Implications." Unpublished dissertation, Ohio State Univesity.

HOFSTADTER, D.R. (1979). "Godel, Escher, and Bach: An Eternal Golden Braid." New York: Basic Books.

KELLY, G.A. (1963). "A Theory of Personality: The Psychology of Personal Constructs." New York: Norton.

LERNER, D. (1958). "The Passing of Traditional Society." New York: Free Press.

LEVI-STRAUSS, C. (1963). "Structural Anthropology." New York: Basic Books.

PEARCE, W.B., and CRONEN, V.E. (1980). "Communication, Action, and Meaning: The Creation of Social Realities." New York: Praeger.

PLATT, G.M. (1980). "Recent Issues in Interpretive Sociology: The Case of Ethnomethodology." (Unpublished manuscript, University of Massachusetts, Amherst.)

RAUSCH, H.L., BARRY, W.A., HERTEL, R.K., and SWAIN, M.A. (1974). "Communication Conflict and Marriage." San Francisco, Jossey-Bass.

SCHUTZ, A. (1964-1971). "Collected Papers." 3 vols. The Hague: Martinus Nyhoff.

TYLOR, E.B. (1929). "Primitive Culture," Vol. 1. (Reprint of 1871 ed.) London: J. Murray.

WEBER, M. (1947). "The Theory of Social and Economic Organization." Trans. by A.M. Henderson and T. Parsons. New York: Free Press.

3

Forced Cooperation:
Violence as a Communicative Act

LINDA M. HARRIS
University of Connecticut
Storrs, Connecticut 06268

ALISON ALEXANDER
University of Massachusetts
Amherst, Massachusetts 01002

SHEILA McNAMEE
University of New Hampshire
Durham, New Hampshire 03824

MARSHA STANBACK
University of Southern Mississippi
Hattiesburg, Mississippi 39406

KYUNG-WHA KANG
Cleveland State University
Cleveland, Ohio 44115

> Once in existence . . . a pattern has a causal efficacy of its own, exerting influence on other aspects of culture, personality and social organization of a society . . . for about 1 out of every 4 couples in the U.S. there has been a recurring pattern of physical violence. (Straus, 1977)

Many current models of domestic violence have dichotomized the individual and the culture in an attempt to explain why violence occures in the context of family life. Psychological models suggest that violence reflects an aggressive, obsessive, or neurotic individual (Straus, 1974). Sociological models blame the desparate social structure of the culture (Straus, 1977), most citing the uneven distribution of a patriarchal family structure. Others claim that the content of our belief system encourages violence by labeling it as a tool for demonstrating love (e.g., when parents punish their children). While both models have been useful in helping us realize that loved ones *do* physically abuse each other, they offer little understanding of the nature of violent patterns or the link between the individual and his/her cultural habitat.

CULTURAL LOGICS

Current models of domestic violence typically view physical violence as inherently disruptive to the usual stability of the family. From a communication perspective, physical violence is seen as sometimes disruptive, other times constructive, but always a sobering symptom of an inherently problematic and frighteningly fragile cultural logic.

Cultural logic exists in the minds of its members. A specific cultural procedure for knowing (e.g., physical punishment helps children "know" right from wrong) exists in the minds of members of a society, club, family, or dyad. Each culture is contained within a larger culture or cultures and is self defined by its own procedures for knowing and acting.

A culture which structures procedures for knowing and acting in a "logic" which contradicts or denies the capacity for human knowledge is inherently problematic. For example, a culture which employs violence to eliminate violence has structured its procedures for knowing and acting in a self-defeating manner.

Symbolic and Brute Force

Symbolic systems are precarious. All *social* forms of communication require a shared or coordinated cultural logic. By refusing to operate within the cultural logic, any individual can deny the very existence of the intended meaning of a symbolic act (i.e., "I'm sorry" can be denied as an apology by any individual involved by not acknowledging it as an act of apology). Thus, the "force" of all social acts depends upon cooperation (see Austin, 1962).

One of the classic examples of symbolic denial is reported by Bateson et al. (1956, p. 18). It concerns a young man who was recuperating from an acute schizophrenic episode in a hospital. During a visit from his mother he embraced her and she stiffened. After withdrawing his arm, she questioned his love for her. He blushed and she reprimanded him for denying his feelings. Within a few minutes after his mother left, the patient physically assaulted an aid.

Their symbolic cultural logic had failed them. They were unable to coordinate a procedure for "knowing" frustration. The son apparently tried to elicit cooperation from his mother in order to see himself as a loved son, but she denied it with actions of hatred. He tried to escape the symbolic bind into his own "schizophrenic" world, but she followed and refused to allow him an escape from her denial even there. Physical violence was one of the few exits left to acknowledge his frustration.

Specifically, physical violence functions to force cooperation when one's cultural logic fails to provide a symbolic system for knowing and acting cooperatively. Its nature is paradoxical. Its brutishness forces cooperation where cooperation is not forthcoming. But forced cooperation denies the possibility for willing cooperation. An individual forced to acknowledge that a violent act has been directed toward him or her *must* either submit or oppose—neither act is an act of willing cooperation.

Physical acts are structurally different from all other forms of "knowing" in a cultural logic. They are brutish (Pearce and Cronen, 1980) in nature, a part of our physical reality which is "known" through our sensory rather than through our symbolic system. The force of a symbolic act depends upon cooperation to make it shared. The force of a physical act does not. While symbolic acts can be denied or ignored, physical acts cannot. They *demand* interpretation or explanation but do not require a shared or coordinated symbol for their existence. (Try *not* making sense out of a physical act directed toward you, much less a physically harmful one.)

In summary, symbolic and brute forces interact in such a way that their strengths and weaknesses play off each other. The shared knowledge of a symbolic act is dependent upon cooperation, but the cooperation *may* take the form of denying the existence of a particular act. The existence of a brutish act cannot be denied, but its existence denies the possibility for willing coooperation. For good or ill, their recurring interplay locks members of a culture into their patterns for knowing and acting.

This paper is about the ills of being trapped in potentially dysfunctional symbolic logics. Bateson's example of a son and his mother bound to their own contorted logic only suggests the ugliness of such entrapment. For even the boy's violent attempt to break out was probably defined by mother, hospital staff, and, tragically, himself, as definite "proof" of his "sickness." There is no exit from *within* a violent bind.

THE COMMUNICATION SYSTEM

Violence is not uncommon nor is it limited to "sick" individuals. Domestic violence is more prevelant than street violence. Two million men and 1.8 million women are physically violated by their spouses each year (Straus et. al., 1980). Most children are violated (often in the form of physical punishment) in this country. Ironically, Straus' discovery of the brute facts of physical violence in millions of families prohibits its denial (in the form of overlooking its significance by social scientists) and forces researchers to re-examine the family communication system. Upon such re-examination it is now apparent that the participants in violent patterns are victims of some of the fundamental flaws of the communication system.

The Inherent Communication Gap

There still exists in our cultural logic a counter-productive myth about communication. Many people, social scientists not excluded, think of communication as a verb—something people *do to* each other. Perfect communication is thought to be possible through the development of speaking and listening skills and commitment to relationships. Thus, imperfect communication—a gap—is created when one person cannot or will not give, try, say, do, "cooperate" enough to meet the other person's needs. It is sometimes difficult to realize that many hold such a limited and dysfunctional view of communication.

The "communication gap" is inherent in the system of creating cultural logics. Individuals in relationships with other individuals make messages (in the form of verbal and nonverbal cues) out of their interpretation of the cultural procedures for knowing and acting. They, in turn, make interpretations (in the form of meanings) of those procedures from the messages of others (Pearce, 1976). Thus, the "structuring of knowledge into ways of knowing and acting" and the interpretation of one's cultural logic are in self-reflexive relationship to each other (Pearce and Cronen, 1980). Herein lies the problem. The "gap" between person A and person B represents the inherent impossibility for humans to have complete knowledge of self, other, or the procedures for knowing and acting in the cultural logic they create together. We therefore create cultural logics for knowing and acting to which we have imperfect access.

With *imperfect knowledge* comes *imperfect cooperation*. That is, while we *must* know the intended meaning of the other's act to acknowledge the existence of the act, we can *never* have perfect knowledge of his/her intentions—even if we ask. Ironically, the harder we try to elicit cooperation the more forced it is and the less likely it is to exist in the form of willing cooperation. Physical violence is a dramatic effort to achieve the impossible, i.e., hitting one's husband in an attempt to gain equality makes willing cooperation toward equality impossible. Forced cooperation is the painful paradoxical result.

The gap between person A and person B does not, of course, prohibit communication from occurring. In fact, acknowledgment of the existence of a gap forces us to see communication as a creative process by which *each* individual forms his/her own cultural logic. That is, a person structures knowledge into procedures for knowing and acting. Two or more people can be involved in the process of cocreating a larger cultural logic as long as each can make sense out of the other's actions (Pearce and Cronen, 1980).

Fortunately, perfect communication is not a necessary characteristic of an operable cultural logic. The hundreds of millions of violence-free relationships are evidence of this fact. Some patterns of interaction can be coordinated with little actual agreement regarding the participants' interpretation (Harris et al., 1979).

SYMBOLIC EXCHANGE LOGIC

The communication gap only becomes dysfunctional when it is ignored. Unfortunately, the prevalent communication logic does exactly that. The popular view of communication, has been documented by dozens of researchers who argue that individuals operate within a "symbolic exchange" logic. "Exchange" theorists have speculated that the exchange process describes what people do when they communicate, i.e., they exchange symbolic messages (Foa and Foa, 1972; Gergen, 1969; Homans, 1961; Thibaut and Kelly, 1959). No exchange theorist to our knowledge has viewed this logic as problematic.

Our own research of patterns of domestic violence indicate that people do indeed believe that communication is an exchange process and that their "communication problems" are due to an imperfect balance in the exchange of necessary and desirable commodities. In fact, we discovered among victims and aggressors from a variety of ethnic, economic, and geographic communities a shared cultural exchange logic about how communication operates. We do not think this logic is unique to participants in domestic violence. Rather, we argue that our subjects are among those who are *most* skillful in the use of a cultural logic that is inherently self-destructive.

Rules for Symbolic Exchange

In an exchange logic of communication, symbols are viewed as *commodities* which can be exchanged from person A to person B by the utterances of messages which represent the symbols. That is, love, respect, trust, equality, etc. can be exchanged by offering statements like "I love, respect, trust, am equal to you." The exchange has occurred when the message is stated.

Symbolic commodities are *limited resources* and should be exchanged *reciprocally*. That is, symbols exist empirically and can thereby be accounted for by keeping track of what and how much has been exchanged by whom. Individuals are viewed as having the capacity to willingly exchange or withhold their commodities. To achieve a reciprocal exchange of symbolic commodities, an individual can keep score of the quantity of exchange (Berne, 1964). For instance, if Mary "gives" Jim many affectionate messages and "discovers" that Jim is not "giving" her an equal "share" she may withhold affection until the exchange is once again equal. Perfect communication exists in an intimate relationship when (a), each partner is giving all positive commodities and withholding all the negative commodities; (b), the exchange is reciprocal; and (c), spontaneous (i.e., both partners cooperate in this balancing act willingly).

When perfect communication does not exist, (i.e., someone is giving negative commodities, withholding positive ones, or the exchange is not reciprocal or spontaneous) one or all members of the relationship adjust the balance as Mary did, or try to persuade the other to cooperate more fully in this spontaneous exchange of symbols.

Forced Coooperation

This cultural logic is problematic because (a), it ignores the creative capacity of each partner to interprete messages within their own cultural logic (i.e., the words "I love you" may be interpreted by Mary as an act of commitment but may be viewed by Jim as an effort on Mary's part to elicit more commitment from him); (b), it assumes perfect communication can occur even though complete knowledge of the interpersonal logic is impossible; (c), it treats symbolic acts as if they are tangible commodities which can be shared without joint acknowledgment; (d), its maintenance poses a contradiction— any deviation from perfect communication warrants forced cooperation which makes spontaniety impossible; and (e), efforts directed toward correcting the imperfection develop into a self-propelled escalation or what Watzlawick et al. (1974) call a game without end and Cronen et al. (1979) refer to as unwanted repetitive patterns.

Ironically, those individuals who have incorporated the exchange logic most successfully are those who are most victimized by it. They are the ones who reach, then stretch, its limits by using acts of physical violence to force cooperation.

Unfortunately, we apparently learn an exchange logic very early and learn few alternative logics for managing our relationships. Some of our research on siblings' fights is a sobering reminder of how embedded in our thinking this logic actually is.

LEARNING PROCEDURES FOR DISTRIBUTING JUSTICE

Our communication analysis of violent patterns involved interviews with 11- to 12-year-old children in New Zealand and in Columbus, Ohio. We found in their accounts of and justifications for physical violence the primitive form of an exchange logic. We also found a lot of physical fighting.

Sibling violence is considered by most parents as "annoyance," a "phase," or somewhat "disquieting," but perfectly normal (Straus, 1979). The children themselves viewed violent acts such as hitting, scratching, shoving, and biting as normal. None of our subjects were embarrassed to admit that they had fought over such things as who gets to select television programs. Thus physical violence is incorporated into the cultural logic early on and, at worst, considered an unpleasant but sometimes necessary communicative act.

Ihinger (1975) suggests that children learn a system of justice and that the amount of sibling conflict is related to the consistency exhibited by parents in applying the system. Our examination of children's rules for distributing justice suggests the rules they use in negotiating what is "fair" (Blau, 1964) involves a primitive form of an exchange logic in which the commodity *is* tangible; in this case, television viewing time.

The norm of reciprocity (Gouldner, 1960) was operating in the nego-tiating strategies of all the children interviewed. They expected that the commodity would be exchanged fairly. This expectation is illustrated in Fran's account of an episode involving violence: "You watch what you want today and I'll watch what I want tomorrow." Fran's account also demonstrates the score-keeping strategy involved in this logic.

Physical violence was employed by siblings when others did not meet the expectations of willing cooperation in negotiating an equitable system of justice. Forced cooperation seemed to be a small price to pay for maintaining a reciprocal system. In fact, younger siblings also expected to be forced to cooperate. Conflicts over who watched what programs frequently escalated into violence. Parents were often called upon to resolve differences and stop the violence.

The symbolic exchange logic, we believe, is learned quite early in childhood and is used to negotiate the exchange of tangible commodities. Expectation of fairness and reciprocity are incorporated into the child's de-veloping cultural logic. Then fights rarely run out of control, because of their reliance on parental intervention. This logic functions reasonably well in the joint achievement of goals as long as the commodities are tangible and there is someone outside the situation who will stop the escalation.

From our interviews with adults, we find individuals using the same form of exchange logic in their attempts to exchange symbols. (Our subjects treat symbols as if they are tangible objects.) Unfortunately, there is rarely a parent around to stop the escalation involved in forced cooperation.

EXEMPLARY CASES OF VIOLENT PATTERNS

One of the theoretical insights which guided our research on violence is summarized in the introductory quotation by Straus—"patterns have causal efficacy of their own." In fact, this idea is a central theme of the commu-nication theory from which our research methodology emerged (Pearce and Cronen, 1980). We set out to examine the cultural logics of violent patterns by asking subjects to describe their own violent episodes.

Our research strategy consisted of choosing four geographically, eco-nomically, or racially different communities to discover whether a violent pattern was operating across them. Case studies of twenty four victims and aggressors were conducted in Korea, New Zealand, a Black lower-middle class community, and two White middle class communities. Several forms of domestic violence were examined; sibling, spouse, and grandparent-grand-child. A structured, empirically-based interview procedure was employed by each of the four researchers (see Pearce and Cronen, 1980, and Harris and Straus, 1980, for detailed methodological procedures). With the possible exception of the Korean sample, we found victims and aggressors struggling to escape "games without end" involving a shared logic of symbolic exchange.[1]

We have selected three exemplary cases to describe what a violent pattern looks like from the point of view of the participants;[2] an aggressor, a victim, and an aggressor/victim.

Case I: An Aggressor

Don reported conflict episodes with his wife in which he violently pushed her against the wall, bruising her badly. While he does not consider himself a violent person, he reported that he felt *others* expected him to be "tough." This, in fact, was what Don described as the heart of his problem and what he pinpointed as the "cause" of his drinking problems. On the advice of his friends, Don decided that marriage would "balance him." As he described it, "I got married because I needed her (his wife) to let me be in control." By definition, being married was to have control. However, he reported that once he was married he "didn't have to act as if I was in control." Because marriage was equivalent to a secure situation where the man is in control, Don believed that he would no longer need to "prove" himself as "tough" by drinking.

Thus, for Don, the commodity he was seeking was control. He believed that the way to acquire this commodity was through marriage. However, in interaction with his wife Don found that "control" was not easily gained. As he described it, "she comes to me asking for help, saying, in effect, 'control me,' but I know that by helping her, giving her what she wants—controlling her—she is really controlling me." Don has clearly articulated his logical dilemma. This emphasizes the great need he feels to obtain control which only his wife can give him. Yet he realizes now that his wife's "giving" him the power to control negates any control he might have.

Don reported a violent episode in which he returned home very late and very drunk. His wife had been worried because he had taken their 3-year-old daughter with him. Upon his return home, a verbal battle ensued, leading to his wife's attempt to call the police. When Don realized what she was attempting to do, he grabbed the phone out of her hand and violently

---

[1] Upon initial inspection of the Korean data we are uncertain as to how to interpret the results. There are real differences between the Korean and other subjects on some scales. We are not yet clear if these differences are due to problems with the scales on cultural differences we were unable to tap. For the purposes of this report, the Korean data were omitted.

[2] We are reporting only qualitative analysis here. For a quantitative analysis of domestic violence, see Harris and Straus (1980).

pushed her against the wall, bruising her badly. To him, this act was his attempt to gain control over the situation. If he failed now, it would count as one more instance when he failed to prove himself to be "tough." By depending on his wife to *make* him powerful (to put him in control) he was unable to gain that control. His violent act was his desperate attempt to force her to "let" him be in control. Paradoxically, it was tangible evidence of his dependence upon her.

Case II: A Victim

The violent relationship in which Lea was involved also is typified by a logic based on the notion of exchange. Lea, recovering from a broken engagement to another man, described the purpose of her current relationship as twofold: (a), to prove to herself and others that she could "get a man" and thus rebuild her ego; and (b), to have a "good time." She described John, her boyfriend, as insecure and in need of the feeling that he was in control. Because she realized his insecurity and need for control, she said his "attempts at power don't mean anything because I know why he needs to be in control."

The violence occurred when Lea tried to end the relationship. She did so in an indirect way by telling John that she needed "time to think about the relationship." According to Lea, John accurately interpreted her message as an attempt to end the relationship. Thus, he tried to demonstrate his power in their relationship through a series of what Lea labeled "sympathy gaining ploys" and "attempts to gain control."

Lea's description of John's logic fits into the notion of an exchange logic. As she saw the situation, John was trying to "get" power or control from her. In this episode he felt powerless. Thus, she thought he hit her in order to bring her closer to him—in order to gain intimacy. But of course the act of violence was a demonstration of helplessness from her point of view, and gave her a tangible reason (undeniable to both) to leave him.

Case Study III: Aggressor/Victim

Susan described her relationship with her husband as one where she assumed the submissive role early, where being submissive was equated with being desirable. Conversely, being aggressive and assertive counted as being "bitchy."

Susan explained that she would become angry with her husband and mother for teaming up "against" her. (She reported a history of conflict with her mother.) Her greatest frustration occurred as a result of her inability to express her anger, or to confront her husband on this issue, because of the dichotomy created by her meaning rules (submissive/desirable vs. assertive/

undesirable). Thus, Susan reported feeling bound by these rules. Although she had been raised believing that it was "good" to be docile and submissive, Susan said she did not feel this role aided in building her self esteem. Thus, her attempt to break out of this relationally-defined role began with the development of a "positive" self image and acts of independence.

The violent episode Susan recalled involved her attempt to "break out" of the relational definition which kept her in the dependent, submissive role. Reunited with her husband, Richard, after a brief separation, the two had planned a "romantic" evening out. When Richard failed to return home from work at the designated time, Susan became angry. After waiting hours, she set out to find him. As anticipated, she found him drunk with his buddies at the local bar. Upon seeing him, she reported giving him a "dirty look," driving home, and going to bed, locking both the apartment door and the bedroom door behind her. Later that night, Richard came home drunk. Breaking down the bedroom door, he dragged Susan out of bed, causing her to bang her head. He then proceeded to swear at and beat her. She pleaded with him to stop, but the beating continued. Finally, in an act which she described as a "demonstration of anger and revenge," she grabbed his hair, pulled him to the ground, and began beating him. When he regained control, he threw Susan across the room with such force that she broke her nose. Stunned, she ran into the bathroom and locked the door. Richard left.

In this case Susan's attempt to move from a relationship which was jointly defined as dominant/submissive to a new relational definition ("equal") created a game without end. The symbolic commodity she was trying to get from Richard was "equality." However, Susan could not "become equal" unless her husband "gave" her equal status. However, his privileged position of granting or witholding her status makes an equal relationship impossible. (See Harris and Straus, 1980, for a similar logic.)

CONCLUSION

The logics described in the violent episodes reported above take the form of an exchange logic. That is, instead of symbolically creating what "counts as" quality, control, intimacy, etc., actors involved in these episodes report their attempts to get Other to *give* them these symbolic commodities. This type of logic produces an escalating game without end, in that actors report behaving as they do because of the relational definitions they hold. Yet, when they act, they are no longer able to maintain those same relational definitions. As long as they expect Other to "give" them power, they must define their relationships as complementary, with one member of the dyad in the dominant or powerful position. Bateson et al. (1956) describe this same kind of confusion of hierarchically ordered levels of meaning in their theory of schizophrenia. They point out that individuals caught in this type of logical confusion find that any effort to "communicate" the problem binds them further.

As expected, in this exchange logic attempts to communicate one's need or desire for control, power, intimacy, equality, etc., are not successful. These attempts are similar to the well-known paradoxical statement, "Be spontaneous!" If one must be told to be spontaneous, then any efforts at following through are only responses to the command. Similarly, any attempts to get Other to "let me be equal" in what is perceived as an unequal relationship are futile.

If this is the case, then acts of physical violence might be viewed as actors' attempts to break out of this dysfunctional exchange logic. Their verbal attempts to get Other to "make" them powerful often fail. However, physically violent acts can, on a different, more apparent level, be exchanged, and the direct results of physical force may be *physically* assessed (e.g., "I gave you larger bruises than you gave me").

Interviews with each subject are suggestive of the irony of physical violence. Subjects reported simultaneously feeling that they have no other options than to strike out; however, at the same time, hitting their partner did not resolve the unwanted pattern they were caught in. In fact, as with verbal attempts to break out of a dysfunctional logic, these violent communicative acts served only to perpetuate the contradictory nature of their logics by accelerating the escalating game without end.

In summary, we have based our argument on the premise that the communication process is unknown to its participants, inherently flawed, making complete cooperation impossible. Physical violence is a communicative act qualitatively different from symbolic communicative acts. Its "brutishness" is undeniable. When symbolic acts fail to elicit cooperation in the creation of a shared reality, physical violence may be used to "force" cooperation.

The paradoxical nature of forced cooperation makes willing cooperation impossible and, thereby, prohibits the attainment of a shared reality. The "causal efficacy" of violence is brutish. It propels victims and aggressors into a state of powerlessness in employing their own procedures for knowing and acting.

The particular procedure of knowing and acting we found in violent patterns was in the form of an exchange logic which is, according to exchange theorists, a deeply rooted social reality in Western cultures. Ironically, those individuals most "knowledgable" and dependent upon this logic for structuring knowledge with others are the most victimized by its inherent but invisible contradictions.

Thus, participants in violent patterns are tragic figures in their own dramas. They may, however, through their own accounts of violence help researchers understand more about the nature of domestic violence and its relationship to cultural procedures for knowing and acting. Those participants who use physical force to break out of dysfunctional patterns may ultimately help us see into the subtleties and complexities of human interaction. Certainly we have learned much from those who have tried other forms of escape. Some try to escape games without end by creating an alternative private and unfalsifiable reality. This rarely works, because we label them schizophrenics. Others try by responding passively and withdrawing into self-blame. We label them depressed. Many physically internalize the problematic nature of their own cultural logic. They get ulcerative colitis.

Our subjects from several different cultural communities illustrate another escape tactic; lashing outward, forcing the flawed logic to work. They are of course "bad," even "criminal." Tragically, in these cases as in others in which the cultural logic is stretched beyond its capacity, physical violence is a "logical" reaction to an illogical procedure for knowing and acting. If this is true, all members of a violent culture are victims of their own imperfectly structured knowledge.

ACKNOWLEDGMENT

Work on this paper was supported by the Family Violence Research Program at the University of New Hampshire through NIMH grants MH 27557 and T 32 MH15161.

REFERENCES

AUSTIN, J.L. (1962). "How to Do Things with Words." Cambridge, MA: Harvard University Press.

BATESON, G., JACKSON D., HALEY, J., and WEAKLAND, J. (1956). Towards a theory of schizophrenia. *Behavioral Sciences* 1, 151-164.

BERNE, E. (1964). "Games People Play." New York: Grove Press.

BLAU, P. (1964). Justice in social exchange. *Sociological Inquiry 34*, 193-206.

CRONEN, V.E. PEARCE, W.B., and SNAVELY, L. M. (1979). A theory of rule-structure and types of episodes and a study of perceived enmeshment in desired repetitive patterns ("URPs"). *Communication Yearbook 3*, 225-240.

FOA, U.G., and FOA, E.B. (1972). Resource exchange: Toward a structural theory of interpersonal communication. *In* A.W. Siegman and B. Pope (Eds.), "Studies in Dyadic Communication." New York: Pergamon Press.

GERGEN, K. (1969). "The Psychology of Behavior Exchange." Reading, MA: Addison—Wesley.

GOULDNER, A.W. (1960). The norm of receprocity: A preliminary statement. *American Sociological Review 25*, 161-178.

HARRIS, L.M., and STRAUS, M.A. (1980). "Demystifying the Double Bind: Patterned Disorder in Domestic Violence." (Paper presented at the National Conference on Family Relations, Portland, Oregon.)

HARRIS, L.M., CRONEN, V.E., and McNAMEE, S. (1979). "An Empirical Case Study of Communication Episodes." (Paper presented to National Council on Family Relations, Boston, Massachusetts.)

HOMANS, G.C. (1961). "Social Behavior: Its Elementary Forms." New York: Harcourt, Brace, Jovanovich.

IHINGER, M. (1975). A contribution toward a theory of sibling conflict. *Journal of Marriage and The Family 37*, 515-524.

PEARCE, W.B. (1976). The coordinated management of meaning: A rules based theory of interpersonal communication. *In* G. Miller (Ed.), "Explorations in Interpersonal Communication." Beverly Hills, CA: Sage.

PEARCE, W.B., and CRONEN, V. (1980). "Communication, Action and Meaning." New York: Praeger.

STRAUS, M.A. (1974). Cultural and organizational influences on violence between family members. *In* R. Prince and D. Barrier (Eds.), "Configurations: Biological and Cultural Factors in Sexuality and Family Life." New York: D.C. Heath, Lexington Books.

STRAUS, M.A. (1977). A sociological perspective on the prevention and treatment of wifebeating. *In* M. Roy (Ed.), "Battered Women." New York: Van Nostrand Reinhold.

STRAUS, M.A. (1979). "A Sociological Perspective on the Causes of Family Violence." (Paper presented at the American Association for the Advancement of Science, Houston, Texas.)

STRAUS, M.A., GELLES, R.J., and STEINMETZ, S.K. (1980). "Behind Closed Doors: Violence in the American Family." New York: Doubleday/Anchor.

THIBAUT, J.W., and KELLY, H.H. (1959). "The Social Psychology of Groups." New York: John Wiley & Sons.

WATZLAWICK, P., WEAKLAND, J.H., and FISCH, R. (1974). "Change: Principles of Problem Formation and Problem Resolution." New York: W.W. Norton.

4

Media and Art as Cultural Data: Interfacing Cultural Artifacts of Colombia and the United States

DANIEL A. SILVERMAN
Eastern Illinois University
Charleston, Illinois 61920

Through an analysis of how a culture relates to its media-environments, one can bring covert assumptions held by members of a culture to view. The directions which a culture takes are dependent upon their collectively molded media-worldview—a view which regulates ways of being within self-pro-created environmental milieus.

If we define culture as communication and communication as culture, as does Hall (1973, p. 191), the study of culture is the analysis of communication patterns implicit within media environments, patterns which often obscure themselves from members indigenous to a culture. It is hypothesized that insights into culture can be obtained by analyzing externalized communication networks as embodied in the characteristic media of a culture. If members of culture extend their minds, bodies, and/or senses through technology, the analysis of the patterns of communication present within such extensions provides the student of culture with access to data which are more objectifiable, or less susceptible to what Webb et al. (1973, pp. 13-34) have identified in categories as: reactive measurement effects, error from the respondent, varieties of sampling error, the access to content, operating ease, and validity checks. Utilizing the study of media and art characteristic of a culture, the investigator can obtain objectifiable insights into environmental milieus from a unique perspective, and it is maintained that such insight, when cross-validated with other research methods, significantly furthers the course of research into cross-cultural phenomena.

For our purposes, a novel characteristic of the culture of Colombia and one characteristic of the United States were chosen as sources which reflect communication patterns present within the cultures. As a medium, the novel serves as a constant within a world of change. The novel rarely modifies itself through time or space. The alphabet encoded onto the printed page uniformly processes culture by extending the visual sense in space and time. Relatively speaking, the novel is immune to deterioration of its form and content. The novel serves as an outered representation—an historical artifact—of the way in which one person perceived his or her environment at one time, or perceived others within a simulated environment, and the medium itself mediates against editing or revising the form and content by the author if the novel is to retain its identity as a medium called a novel.

The novels chosen for the analyses of culture are Gabriel Garcia Marquez's *One Hundred Years of Solitude* and Ken Kesey's *Sometimes A Great Notion*. One consideration for the selection of the novels as cultural data banks was that of whether they were introspective or extrospective in scope. It was ascertained through the review of the critical literature, from statements made by the authors, and from data obtained from informants in the field, that qualitatively the novels do represent collective authorships within the cultures, i.e., communication patterns as contained in the novels can be generalized to the cultures at large; furthermore, it was ascertained that both Garcia Marquez and Kesey perceptually screened their cultural envelopes and that they exposed their perceptual screens for our perusal through the form and content of the novels.

The focus for this study are the elements of the Primary Message System of Learning (Hall, 1973, pp. 46-52) present within each of the novels. It is maintained that the systems for learning as contained within the two novels serve as a paradigm for the ways in which populations in Colombia and the United States learn.

For our purposes, let learning mean: all that a cultural member assimilates from his other environment which, either consciously or unconsciously, modifies the way in which he or she sees the world; learning, one of the Primary Message Systems as defined by Hall, manifests itself in all of the other nine Primary Message Systems, but it still may be considered on its own (Hall, 1973, pp. 34-39).

Let us peruse, briefly, the Kesey novel, *Sometimes A Great Notion*, relative to learning systems present within it, which will provide us with a foundation with which to compare the Garcia Marquez novel. In the former novel, we have a dramatic conflict presented between two warring factions of the small lumber town of Wakonda—the conflict between the individual and his needs as represented by the Stamper patriarchs, and the group and its felt needs as represented by the townspeople who are members of a logger's union which has called a strike. The Stampers, who are anti-union, have contracted with a lumbermill to supply all needed lumber regardless of the union's strike.

In respect to the role of tradition as a part of the educational environment of a group, we may say that the people of the two fall into a tradition, using the word "tradition" loosely, of falling together into a group for their protection against the external environment and from persons who are not members of the group. The Stamper patriarchs, on the other hand, are part of a tradition which isolates the individual from the group so that he or she can fight the external environment alone. The organizational structure for the maintenance of grouping in the town of Wakonda is what one could consider as a poor excuse for the replacement of the nuclear family, the institution (the union). On the other hand, the Stampers maintain the organizational structure of the nuclear family which utilizes modelling after the dominant patriarch by its members for learning purposes, and is characterized by solidarity of perception by the members who play an active role in the traditions which serve as a base for the organization.

The townspeople and the Stampers, with their polarities, both utilize a given space for the maintenance of the organization—the Snag, a bar frequented by union members, and the Stamper home, respectively. The loose bonding of people in Wakonda parallels the easy access by all to the space; since all persons in the Wakonda area may enter the bar, the Snag becomes a nebulous entity, since its membership is constantly in flux, as is the way in which the group perceives the environment. The Stamper household, on the other hand, assists in the maintenance of group solidarity by limiting significant access to the house to family members.

Within the two poles, different manifestations of learned sexual roles present themselves. The townspeople males of Wakonda never undergo rites of passage from adolescence into maturity. In contrast to this, all three of the Stamper patriarchs have undergone rites of passage—the eldest patriarch's conquering of nature essentially on his own, the second patriarch Hank's constant struggle against other men who attempt to defeat him, and the youngest patriarch Leland's transformation away from embracing woman as mother into maturity and independence. In addition, the femal townspeople represent a fragmented image of woman—woman as temptress and woman as vulture. Within the Stamper household, however, the total woman is represented by the character Viv—woman as temptress, woman as goddess, woman as mother, and woman as facilitator of the rites of passage for her men; however, as with all of the women in the household before her, the Stamper patriarchy expels Viv from its environment.

When the culture of the United States as embodied in Kesey's novel is interfaced with the culture of Colombia as embodied in Garcia Marquez's novel, significant contrasts present themselves. One conspicuous disharmonious element between the novels is the way in which time is structured by the artists. Although Kesey utilizes multi-faceted temporal perspectives toward his action and characters, the dominant system of time in his novel is historical; Garcia Marquez utilizes ahistorical, or mythical, time systems in his novel.

In the Kesey novel, *a* Stamper myth—"never give an inch"—drives the action of the novel forward linearly and sequentially by serving as an impetus for the conflictive action of the novel and for the motivation of the Stamper patriarch's actions. On the other hand, in the Garcia Marquez work, the "mythic" is much more than a background for the development of story—it is a cosmic force which manifests itself repeatedly, in all of its grandeur. For example, Garcia Marquez gives us images of Melquiades the gypsy who is immune to time and to space, the visitations by the ghost of Prudencio Aguilar to the main characters' home, Remedios the Beauty's ascension into heaven, and the image of the town of Macondo which blows away after its one hundred years of existence.

Because of their mythical orientation within time in Macondo, the "new" and "old" there differ radically from the "new" and "old" in Wakonda. Among other differences created by culture, the Stampers and the Buendias substantially differ in ways in which they structure their perspectives of time and in how the educational environments of the families are modified accordingly.

American time is convolutional in nature. The culture's system of time is similar to a vortex in that it begins at point X and spirally ascends to point Y without any contact of the two points. Time in the United States is structured culturally so that it progresses and never returns upon itself. Such directionality is created by the culture's predisposition for the assimilation of the new into it and through the utilization of the new as an indispensable foundation for future directions.

In Kesey's novel the "new" is incorporated into flexible temporal systems held by the novel's characters, a process which is responsible for changes within the systems. Henry accepts logging machinery as a more efficient way to get the work done and he rejects the theory that things were better in the "good old days." Hank lacks the knowledge for logging in the old fashioned way, and requires Henry's advice relative to how it was done in the past. Furthermore, if one were to project the Stamper household into the future, one would necessarily have to modify its direction because of the incorporation of the new embodied in Leland.

As viewed in the Macondo environment, the new is reacted to violently by its recipients, rather than being susceptible to incorporation as it is with the Stampers. For instance, Jose Arcadio Buendia, one of the founders of the town Macondo, is described after his exposure to the great inventions carried by the gypsies:

> That spirit of social initiative disappeared in a short time, pulled away by the fever of the magnets, the astronomical calculations, the dreams of transmutation, and the urge to discover the wonders of the world. From a clean and active

man, Jose Arcadio Buendia changed into a man lazy in appearance, careless in his dress, with a wild beard that Ursula managed to trim with great effort and a kitchen knife. There were many who considered him the victim of some strange spell.

In Macondo, the new is reacted to violently by its recipients. The reactions vary from the person's alienation from reality to his rejection of the media. In addition, the two cultures vary considerably in the respect that in the United States media are an integral part of cultural life and their introduction does not create violent reactions; on the other hand, in Colombia as represented by the community of Macondo, because of the unique character of the introduced media and because there were few previous introductions of media, the media are usually rejected and when they are embraced they destroy elements of the traditional culture.

Rather than time moving linearly and sequentially as it does in Kesey's novel, the time in *One Hundred Years of Solitude* is cyclical; there is no way of defining the present, as there is no way of differentiating the future from the past. For instance, Ursula, the matriarchial force behind the maintenance of the family, is obsessed with the belief that events repeat themselves over and over again, much as a record player repeats the same song over and over again.

In short, the Colombian and American systems of time, as represented in the two novels, are significantly different. Colombian time may be seen as a cycle which repeatedly returns upon itself; the cyclic temporal system may move in directions and then return to a previous point in time or it deceptively may appear to move when in reality it is stationary, as demonstrated by the times of solitude of the Buendias. On the other hand, in the United States, time moves along the patch of its vortex and never returns upon itself because of the system's incorporation of new media into it, which changes its structure.

The action of the Garcia Marquez novel occurs primarily within an extremely restricted physical space—the Buendia household. The sustaining force behind the action of the novel is the successful procreation and maintenance of the integrated household-family unit. Though various family members leave the homestead for various reasons, their return is always present. Understanding the novel is dependent upon comprehending that the Buendia household is an extension of the collective Buendia familial mind—that mind being the nucleus around which all other phenomena constellate.

Previously we discussed the Stamper household as metaphorically descriptive of the Stampers' battle for life against nature. The Stampers' relationship with nature was one of conflict between man on the inside of his house against vicious nature on the outside. Though the Buendias' relationship with nature is in some ways similar to that of the Stampers', the delineation of the conflict differs.

Rather than the Buendia polarization from the ravages of nature being one of inside-outside, it is one of the inside equalling the outside. The Buendia survival problem is one of maintaining the harmony and health of the family within the home, rather than to the outside elements. The polarization of family members inevitably creates, and is manifested in, the destruction of the physical house itself. The aberrational processes within the minds of the family members create havoc within the total household-family environment. In general, it can be said that when the fragmentation of the mystique of the home occurs, the house disintegrates.

The actions of the characters in the novel present a battle between those ideals of the culture embodied in Ursula the matriarch, and informally taught by her, with the neglect of those ideals as embodied in the men with their implicit rejection of the needs of the group. Ursula, the carrier of culture, serves as a planet who attempts to keep her star-children within her orbit. It is hypothesized that the learning system most engendered by the members of the culture of Colombia for the maintenace of culture is that of modelling personality after the dominant matriarch within an extended family group. The matriarch Ursula keeps the home intact in spite of the idiocy of her sons who follow after the model of their father. Ursula serves as a pragmatist in the house of male dreamers.

In summary, the Stampers and the Buendias are representatives of the cultures of the United States and Colombia. The ways in which they perceive their worlds have been molded by their cultural milieus. They see and interact with their worlds as their milieus have programmed them to do so. A part of the way in which they see their worlds is the way they have learned to learn their relationship with their environment.

The Stampers, who are able to carry on the Stamper tradition of never giving an inch, are those in the family who adopt the tradition by being one with it. It is a system of adaptation learned by Henry from his environment, learned by Hank from his father, learned by Leland from his father, from his brother, and from his environment. All of the characters in the novel who are unable to fit into the environment by means of the tradition are spat out of the environment into milieus which are similarly uncomfortable for them.

The tradition of the Buendias is embodied in the matriarch Ursula. The word *tradition* is used to signify the presence of a perceptual field which is capable of handling environmental phenomena through its mastery of the same. The adoption of the stance taken by the Buendia men fails to be a tradition, because of the stance's incapacity to meet environmental pressure head-on. The men of the family model themselves after the other men in the family, so that they all share withdrawal from the world into worlds of their own making. The tradition carried by Ursula is carried with her into her coffin, and the rest of her line are carried off by the wind.

The Stamper house is representative of the myth behind the Stampers—conquer. It fights nature as do the men within it. The myth, when remembered, pushes the men into victory over all which threatens them. The Stamper house is the Stamper man.

The Buendia house is a battleground. Within it, the matriarchally carried tradition combats all who desires to destroy it. The chaos within the house represents the chaos within the total family organization. The house, as that of the Stampers, is built with hope, but, unlike the Stampers, blows away because hope blows away.

The Stampers are oriented around their tradition. The Buendias are given one hundred years of life because of the matriarchal tradition embodied in Ursula. The Stamper men spit out the female elements in the home; Ursula unsuccessfully attempts to attract the men who spit themselves out of the tradition of the home.

The Stamper tradition is that of the individual conquering all in his wake so that he can realize his individuality. The individual models himself after another individual, so that he is able to fall into the tradition as represented by his model. The Stamper tradition is characterized by its transmittal informally, and by the absence of both formal and technical learning (Hall, 1973, pp. 68-72).

Ursula's tradition is taught in the hope that others will learn from her informally. Her tradition is characterized by the absence of both formal and technical learning. She models herself after the group of women who came before her and who will come after her—the tradition of matriarchs of which she is a part. Ursula has modelled well; her students fail to learn the environmental importance of modelling after her.

Time in the United States is convolutional; time in Colombia is cyclical. Ursula's tradition, which was neglected in her lifetime, would again be reborn and would die. Ursula's tradition would manifest itself in women who serve the culture as she served it, whereas the Stamper tradition would never again be the same. The Stamper tradition modifies as do the individuals who embody it; Ursula's tradition is part of a collective history which does not distort because of the environmental necessity for it to remain as a constant.

References

HALL, E.T. (1973). "The Silent Language." Garden City, New York: Anchor.
WEBB, E.J., CAMPBELL, D.T., SCHWARTZ, R.D., and SECHREST, L. (1973). "Unobtrusive Measures." Chicago, IL: McNally.

5

Cultural Predispositions of Mexican Amercians: A Rhetorical Experiment in Textual Criticism

AL GONZALEZ
The Ohio State University
Columbus, Ohio 43200

The prevailing theories of cosmic dynamics depict a constantly expanding universe. Though essentially empty, this universe is occasionally occupied by matter, as is readily apparent in our awareness of this earth and the planets, the sun, and the distant galaxies. Sometimes, these galaxies of matter collide, with their physical and gravitational properties determining the degree of disruption each will experience. The expansive spiral galaxies, for example, seem to pass through one another unscathed, while the denser elliptical galaxies suffer cataclysmic distortion.

The human being is a galaxy of ideas, beliefs, habits, and material possessions which, having been learned from and shared with others, constitutes membership in a culture. Yet we know that there are various cultures; so the opportunity for "collisions" among members of different cultures exists. The task for scholars of rhetoric, then, is not unlike that of the astronomer: first, to develop an instrument which makes visible the object of study (i.e., a methodology which brings into relief rhetorical strategies as cultural indicants) and, second, to understand the implications of identified forces, more precisely to comprehend the convergence and interaction of different sets of tacitly ascribed symbolic meanings.

The intent of this study is to advance and apply a means for the rhetorical criticism of campaigns by collectives when conflicting cultural influences are seen as being significantly problematic. Specifically, the conflicting cultural "galaxies" examined here radiate from interactions between the Mexican American world imagination of migratory farmworkers in Ohio with the world imagination of the majority or "Anglo" culture represented by Ohio farmers, produce processors, and the general public. The analysis proceeds in three steps. First, a methodology for the study of culture and communication is developed using a literary "text" metaphor; second, major traits of the historical-culture character of Mexican predispositions are abstracted from the cultural critiques of Octavio Paz; and third, the textual approach and the Mexican predispositions are applied to the campaign of militant nonviolence waged by the Mexican-American Farm Labor Organizing Committee (FLOC) of northwest Ohio.

1.

The purpose of this section is to outline a framework for the cultural analysis of rhetoric. Conceptions of culture seem to include the total life patterns apparent in the learned and taught conversations, values, language, and material tools of a people. Moreover, Prosser (1978, p. 5) states, that "communication and culture are so closely bound together that virtually all human social interaction is culturally linked." Given this perspective, a cultural conceptualization of rhetoric becomes not only possible, but extremely helpful. Carey (1975 p. 13) has suggested, rhetoric can be viewed as the process of incorporating tacitly held collective meanings in the symbolic production, maintenance, and transformation of reality. This view shifts the focus of rhetorical criticism from the explicitly deliberated surface meanings of messages to the deeply pervasive, culturally-rooted intentions and constructions which underlie messages and describe a particular world view.

What critical methodology, then, does this cultural definition of rhetoric suggest? As a starting point, we consider the following observation by Hall (1976, p. 37):

> What is characteristically man . . . is his culture, the total communication framework: words, actions, postures, gestures, tones of voice, facial expressions, the way he handles time, space, and materials. . . . All these things and more are complete communication systems with meanings that can be read correctly only if one is familiar with the behavior in its historical, social and cultural context.

First, words are not the only conveyors of meaning. The *way* people do things communicates also. If we consider technology to be any manner in which humans alter their environment as a response to a problem or desire, then special forms of such adaptation can be considered cultural messages. The fact that, say, a Mexican American is able to use a hand-baked tortilla first to place food on, next as an eating utensil, and then finally to eat the tortilla as part of the meal, whereas the Anglo American uses separately a plate, a spoon (none of which are likely to have been produced in the home), is among other things a telling statement of Mexican self-containment versus Anglo self-expansion. This technological difference becomes a cultural message, the interpretation of which may suggest the nature of tacit knowledge that channels experience into "reality."

Also, Hall notes three aspects of human behavioral context: the historical, social, and cultural. The social aspect of communicative behavior refers to the surface meanings attributed in everday interaction, the historical aspect recognizes the process/developmental nature of cultural predispositions, and the cultural aspect includes the influence of these collectively-taken-for-granted predispositions which are invisible in most everyday interaction. From this, three methodological operations are suggested: (a), to discover the significant historical remnants which give meaning in the cultural milieu; (b), to identify those predispositions or tacit understandings which seem to have been translated from cultural history to cultural present; and (c), to determine the forms these predispositions have given to the symbolic reality of the rhetor.

These three operations provide the foundation for a textual analysis of rhetoric because, as Hall implies above and as Carey (1975a, p. 187) makes clear:

> A cultural science of communication . . . views human behavior, or more accurately human action, as a text. Our task is to construct a "reading" of the text. The text itself is a sequence of symbols-speech, writing, gesture-that contain interpretations. Our task, like that of a literary critic, is to interpret the interpretations.

Our operations attempt to become familiar with the rhetorical "text" of technological and verbal action symbols by checking its "authenticity" or past, its predominant "themes" or meanings, and its unique "vocabulary" or expression. It is possible also to reverse this order and work back from the social aspect to the historical. The salient feature, however, is not so much the order of the operations as it is the qualitative differentiation of symbolic meaning within the human behavioral context.

Since, ultimately, we wish to read the campaign text of FLOC, whose leadership and membership is mostly Chicano, it becomes necessary to gain some insight into the cultural history of this group. This is the task of section 2.

2.

What are the significant historical remnants which have given and are giving a world imagination or meaning for the farmworkers in northwest Ohio, and what are the cultural predispositions (or sentiments) which seem to have been translated from this cultural history to the cultural present? Here, we may look at the historical cultural experience of the migrants, in relation to Mexico and the United States, not under any pretense of detailing their past, but merely to suggest the cultural *process* in which these people and their predecessors have participated. Also, while not attempting to define the Mexican American psyche or character, we may infer some of the interpretations of reality which FLOC members bring to and suggest in their campaign rhetoric. Again, as a starting point I refer to Hall (1976, p. 4). He notes that "most cultures and institutions they engender represent highly specialized solutions to rather specific problems." What problems and solutions have the Mexicans responded to which help to account for their culture?

> Early man in America was a hunter, a food gatherer, and sometimes a fisherman. Contrary to recent popular assertions, his prominent trait was not aggressiveness but insecurity. It must be supposed that man spent an inordinate amount of his time merely struggling to survive and was almost constantly on the search for food. For thousands of years, the Indian led a precarious existence, with no perceptible improvement in his condition (Meyer and Sherman, 1973, p. 26).

A new way of life did come to America. During the height of the Classic period of pre-Columbian Mexico (200 B.C.–800/1000 A.D.) The need to feed a mass population, and therefore to determine the crucial planting cycles, led to a development of "precise calendrical markings from an established mathematical system" (Meyer and Sherman, 1973, p. 15). Nevertheless, these scientists did not make use of metals or the wheel. Though theoretically capable of immense technological achievement, it was culturally precluded by a "fundamental Mexican trait—the subordination of technical perfection to the irresistible propensity for the aesthetic," (Meyer and Sherman, 1973, p. 16).

The Spanish conquest of Mexico and the subsequent mixture of Spanish and Indian blood introduced a new minority to the scene: the Mestizo. The Spanish government of the early 16th Century viewed the people of the New World as equal candidates for Heaven or Hell, and so took the responsibility for their Christianization (Nava, 1973, p. 26). Adopting elements from both cultures, the Mestizo came to value work, but did not see this as the purpose in life. Nava (1969, p. 48) states, "A man worked in order to have what was more important to him—leisure to do what he wanted. Conversation with pleasant company, a long meal with the family, dancing or relaxation were at least as important as working." Yet farmworkers in 19th Century Mexico were subjugated to the hacienda and held to their European bosses by debt. The average farm wage remained stable throughout the century—at about 35 centavos per year (Meyer and Sherman, 1979, p. 461).

During the 19th and early 20th Centuries, immigration to the U.S. was not restricted at the southern border. The general shortage of domestic labor resources during the Civil War and World Wars I and II encouraged the northward flow of Mexicans in search of work (Nava, 1969, p. 48). Many Mexicans came across as unskilled laborers and were forced to follow the harvest crops. The variable climate of the Northern states determined that farmers rely on seasonal labor, and, during the harvest periods, the "hired hand" came to be regarded as "an integral though lowly member of rural society" (Schob, 1975, p. 1). As agricultural technology boomed in the 20th century, the identities of nature and the farmworker became sublimated to the concerns of the grower. Subsequent generations of Mexican laborers, as U.S. citizens, continue as migrant farmworkers.

The prehistoric and historic insecurity of Mexican life figures largely in modern interpretations of Mexican world views. Contemporary Mexican poet-philosopher Paz (1961) looks at Mexican history to describe his country's cultural predispositions. Historically, the natural ferocity of the Mexican desert, the jungle, and the mountain have created such an uncertainty of existence that centuries of sudden trauma have not faded from cultural memory. In addition, Mexico has come under the politico-cultural domination of France, Spain, and the United States. Even if existence were guaranteed, ideological identity would not be. Thus, as Paz observes, the Mexican "wants to go back beyond the catastrophe he suffered, beyond the orphanhood of having been torn from the all." Here, the seminal Mexican predisposition is defensive in nature. The Mexican "closes-in" as an attempt to go back, inside, to contemplate within the self the waiting, approaching eternity in which commune the original connections of Mexico. Often, according to Paz, the anguish of loss explodes in the form of violent and confused celebration. Just as often, the anguish simmers in the guise of social affectation and pretense.

As a participant-observer of the culture, Paz (1961, p. 20) deep-structures Mexican surface behavior into three general traits: Hermeticism, Dissimulation, and Fiesta. Hermeticism refers to the protective posture of the individual, a closing up and hiding away of the self as construed by the individual. This "true" self can hide in subservience to religious ritual and love of form in daily routine, and in exaggerated attention to etiquette. Dissimulation furthers the hermetic sentiment when the individual transposes the true self with a new, "invented" self which is not hidden. The Fiesta is another escape. It suspends the insecurity of life to allow a release from the "silence and reticence" which predominate Mexican moods. Celebrations of color and movement provide transitions between cycles of resignation and renewal.

The suspicion, the artifice and drollery, and the extravagance so characteristic, as surface behavior of Mexicans and, by extension, of U.S. Mestizos, can only be comprehended when one recognizes the profound ambivalence with which the Mexican approaches life. The symbolic images in ancient and recent myths, architecture, dance, ritual, etc., constitute the reality of Mexican life-as-combat. The irony in the "solitude" of the Mexican is the symbolic richness and totality of consubstantiality-producing participation with which it is sustained.

Despite the influence of acculturation, some measure of Pazean "Mexican-ness" can be detected in the living of Mestizo farmworkers in the U.S. Interestingly, Friedland and Nelkin (1971, pp. 1-2) describe three predominant themes of contemporary migrant life: disorganization and unpredictability (what Paz calls Fiesta), detachment (what Paz calls Hermeticism), and adaptive behavior (what Paz calls Dissimulation). The Mestizo migrant carries a galaxy of cultural sentiments, as does the Anglo-American grower. How do these sentiments exert themselves in farmworker rhetoric? Too, what does an examination of the rhetorical ramifications of these sentiments reveal about the nature of the farmworker/grower conflict in Ohio? A rhetorical-textural analysis of the Mestizo campaign of the Farm Labor Organizing Committee (FLOC) is considered below.

3.

A description of FLOC and its activities has been withheld for heuristic reasons to preserve the focus of our prior steps. Some of the particularly salient historical and cultural aspects of Mexican reality have been considered. Now, at the social level, we can seek the evidence for the influence of the Hermetic, Dissimulatory, and Festive predispositions in a specific rhetorical effort.

Several factors contribute to the attractiveness of FLOC as a case for study. First, in contrast to the migrant workers in California, the social plight of the seasonal workers in Ohio and their rhetorical effort to improve this condition have gone largely unreported. Second, FLOC is a multi-dimensional organization whose varied instruments of persuasion challenge a theoretical framework for the study of cultures. Finally, FLOC is an ongoing, contemporaneous movement which does not limit investigation solely to an historical perspective. The implications of a critical assessment may provide valuable insights into conflict resolution.

FLOC has been in existence since Baldemar Velasquez "walked out of the tomato field one day in 1967 and decided the migrants needed a union" (Rose, 1979). Velasquez and his Toledo-based staff claim a membership of 3,500 migrants from Ohio, Texas, Florida, and California. The organization perceives two situations which contribute to the intolerability of the status quo. First, there is the situation of the farmworker: 15-hour work days with no minimum wage, the subsequent encouragement and widespread use of child labor, camp housing which is dilapidated and inadequate, the absence of any medical coverage and transportation benefits, and the absence of a forum in which these needs can be communicated and negotiated directly with the growers and processors. Second, there is the "million dollar" profit-taking by the tomato processors—specifically, Campbell Soup Co. (located in Napolean) and Libby (located in Leipsic)—and their unresponsiveness to FLOC's demands for negotiation.

For their own convenience, Campbell and Libby view the migrants as employees of the growers and "will not inject [ourselves] into the labor negotiations between our suppliers and others with whom they have contractual relations" (Rose, 1979). Thus, the processors see no obligation to respond to labor demands or even acknowledge that the migrants are the primary workers. The growers, on the other hand, cite the 7-dollar per ton markdown in the price Campbell was willing to pay for tomatoes in 1979, as evidence that growers are unable to grant labor demands.

In the harvest periods since 1978, FLOC has struck the tomato crops in Putnam and Henry Counties. On September 4, 1978, and again on August 25, 1979, Velasquez led scores of workers on 4-day marches to dramatize strike efforts. On January 28, 1979, FLOC announced a national boycott of all Campbell and Libby products. Violence between farmworkers and growers has increasingly accompanied FLOC activities.

Though our analysis of FLOC attempts to connect its union rhetoric with a Mexican world view, we must take time to note that the Anglos will react to FLOC appeals in ways deep-structured by their own culture. The nature of local Anglo reaction to FLOC has been hostility and resistance. What relevant predispositions are identifiable on the Anglo side?

With reference to agriculture, Shover (1976, p. 1) reports that "America's experience with the frontier had fortified two of the most important ingredients of the national character, nationalism and individualism." The early farmer had a duty to build the country and this required a management of nature. The land had been parceled into townships, and within each were smaller units of productivity known as family farms.

A present-day consequence of this ingrained nationalism is that the grower must participate in, or utilize, the technological advances of society; America *is* technology. Simultaneously, the notion of individualism facilitates a possessiveness of the land, and the need for private control and fulfillment of purpose and resolve in all dealings with it. Very generally now, we can hypothesize that (a), at the level of cultural predispositions, the Anglo exalts the self while the Mestizo deemphasizes the self; and that (b), these differing perspectives may potentially hinder understanding between the cultures.

With the Anglo sentiments of nationalism and individualism in mind, we turn more directly to a "reading" of the FLOC campaign for increased farmworker benefits.

Although this analysis discusses the general symbolic output of FLOC, our focus is the first farmworker convention, on August 4, 1979, in Holgate, Ohio, to organize the second strike of the tomato harvest. Along with Velasquez, featured speakers were Tom Nowel of the American Federation of State, County, and Municipal Employees, and Cesar Chavez of the United Farmworkers of America.

The Hermetic deep-structure is suggested by the conspiracy myth[1] repeatedly incorporated into FLOC's persuasive appeals. Velasquez (1979) stated:

> We have had conspiracies already mounting with the sheriff of Putnam County and other people. He admitted . . . that he was going door to door to each labor camp asking the workers to sign a petition saying they don't want in the camp. With the law on the side of the canneries, it's very difficult. So, that's why the strike, the boycott and the solidarity of the workers is even more important.

And:

> There's one driver, sooner or later we'll get to know him better, who admitted to us that one grower paid him $5,000 to bring the people he now has in his fields. And beside that, he loaned him $7,000 to loan to the people to pay their expenses to come up. He was asking if FLOC could do this. As we were leaving, one of the farmers came up to him and said, "Good boy, good boy, you did a good job."

Nuestra Lucha, the official FLOC publication, often reports exploitation, cross burnings, airplane surveillance, and rumors of threats directed at FLOC. (Strike prompts harassment, 1979). The suspicion of the Mestizo functions to create a distance between the individual and a potential danger. While the rhetorical effect of this displayed suspicion may well recruit some sympathizers and strengthen member unity, it may have the net effect of keeping growers and migrants apart and of damaging FLOC's overall credibility with the general public. The key to understanding this "distancing" lies in distinguishing the predispositions of both parties toward conspiracy. The Mestizo uses the conspiracy myth to withdraw, to close in and maintain security (or solidarity). The Anglo response to conspiracy is aggressive in purpose. The conspiracy is viewed as a threat to personal control which must be confronted. Watergate and the Kennedy assasination are exemplary instances of governmental and news media aggression (in the form of investigation and reform) in response to the North American's fascination with conspiracy. The Anglo will interpret FLOC's conspiracy themes as attacks, while the Mestizo will recognize these themes as acknowledgements to an unmitigated fate.

---

[1]"Myth" is accepted here as "A credible, dramatic, socially constructed re-presentation of perceived realities that people accept as permanent fixed knowledge of reality while forgetting . . . its tentative, imaginative, created, and perhaps fictional qualities" (Nimmo and Combs, 1980, p. 16).

Dissimulation is detected by the myth of "sacrifice." Recall that, in Dissimulation, the true self is hidden by an exposed "substitute" self. All "true" members of FLOC are martyrs. The farmworkers have only their labor, and that is withheld for the strike. The only meaning in life is gained through sacrifice to the strike. Fernando Cuevas (1980), speaking at Ohio State University, relates to Ohio, to picketing, and he even decided not to return to his other job in Texas so that he could help FLOC. He "doesn't know" how his family "survived." Speaking to the FLOC delegates, Chavez states:

> The men, women and children who work in the fields, because they're exploited, because they don't have an instrument to bring about economic justice for themselves . . . are responsible for the food we eat . . . It seems to me, that if these people are willing to sacrifice themselves to do this vital, vital work, then the public should be helping them.

FLOC (1979) protests the "poverty lifestyle" and "devastation" of the workers and seeks to struggle for their "basic human needs." Velasquez frequently speaks of every generation from child to grandmother having to stoop in the fields just to survive. The true self is drawn back behind a pathetic, sacrificial desire. The dramatic expressions of Dissimulation provide a comfortable reality for the Mestizo; the historical experience of the Mexican have made sacrifice and adversity totally expected.

Yet, for the Anglo, the hyperbole of Dissimulation has the effect of making FLOC's demands totally and unconditionally warranted. How can a management negotiate downward a *minimum* wage for a *devastated* people? There is little to recommend, from a management viewpoint, entering into this kind of bargaining setting where unilateral concession (i.e., loss of control) is predetermined. The irony here is that the Mestizo's defensive exaggeration is a genuine indication of underlying social tensions.

Finally, the Fiesta attitude is often present in FLOC appeals, e.g. by Velasquez (1980):

> All's we got is our lives—the labor that we're doing, we're tired of giving it away cheaply. So we're going to employ ourselves to work for the boycott, to work for the strike, which is more fun than picking tomatoes anyway. So we're going to have a good time—we come to Columbus here, we go all over the place. Shoot, we tell people to join FLOC and see the world, migrants!

And again, Velasquez (1980) describes FLOC's first job action:

> We put our picket line in the front yard of the biggest grower in Lucas County, John Ackerman. The line got bigger and bigger and bigger; the crowd came more into his yard until we took up all of his yard. People brought these things that you barbeque on, the churches were bringing hotdogs, and then a Mariachi band showed up from Erie, Michigan, and we had a continuous program. In three days, we signed twenty-two contracts.

During the summer months, FLOC functions are often conducted under big-top tents. Food and children are rarely restricted during these functions. The consequent atmosphere is disarmingly informal.

The farmworker convention was no exception to the Festival deep-structure. It was a time for business, gaiety, and generosity. When the passing of resolutions became tedious, business was abruptly suspended so the Mariachi band could play. Children were periodically sent into the sections for the delegates, audience, and press, bearing boxes of fruit. When the burritos were ready in the tent behind the convention hall, Velasquez immediately proclaimed a luncheon recess.

Dismissing sacrifice, the Anglo must perceive a certain randomness and a "less-than-total-effort" from the Festival aspects of the FLOC campaign, which may incorrectly suggest insincerity and contempt toward farming. It may be this culturally perceived indirection which is most resisted, for it threatens the strength of the individual and, by extention, of the country as well. From the Anglo view, only when FLOC finds the *will* to succeed, will the farmworkers "deserve" an improvement, even though this need not be welcomed.

The Fiesta is an effective counterweight to both the suspicion of Hermeticism and the militancy of Dissimulation. Being personal is mixed with reserve, and this basic duality is what FLOC would bring to the negotiation table. The opportunity for misunderstanding would be great when confronting a perspective sensitized to opposites instead of complements. Bernard L. Erven (1979), Professor of Agricultural Economics at Ohio State University remarks, "What is FLOC trying to do? It doesn't act like a bargaining agent. It's a beautiful social services group. Are they naive? No. Why don't they behave like a union?" Social services, a personal trait of the Festival, and the strike, an element of Hermetic reserve and suspicion, cannot easily be reconciled in the Anglo mind, because they are not ready for what they are: pre-Columbian solutions to 20th-century uncertainty.

CONCLUSION

The goal of this study has been to illuminate the conflicts of interpretation regarding the symbolic interactions between a primarily Mexican-American organization and its Anglo-American audience in terms of their underlying cultural sentiments. The description of deep-structured cultural meanings developed from surface behavior seen in the rhetorical campaign of the Farm Labor Organizing Committee is meant as an example of rhetorical-textual criticism. The major rhetorical problem for FLOC is seen to be the creation, for the Anglo, of an accurate perception of its motives.

This study has not meant to portray FLOC as solely a "little Mexico" in Ohio. Certainly, many adaptations to the Anglo culture have been made. Future study is needed to show how these adaptations occur, and how they are in evidence.

REFERENCES

CAREY, J. W. (1975a). Communication and culture. *Communication Research, 2,* 173-191.

CAREY, J. W. (1975b). A cultural approach to communication. *Communication 2,* 1-22.

CHAVEZ, C. (1979). (Talk to FLOC delegates, Aug., Holgate, Ohio.)

CHUEAS, F. (1980). (Speech at Ohio State University, Jan. 23, Columbus, Ohio.)

ERVEN, B. L. (1979). (Personal interview, Ohio State University Agriculture Campus, Nov. 30.)

FLOC. (1979). (Letter to the membership, Jan. 19.)

FRIEDLAND, W. H., and NELKIN, D. (1971). "Migrant." New York: Holt, Rinehart and Winston.

HALL, E.T. (1976). "Beyond Culture." Garden City, New York: Anchor Press/ Doubleday.

MEYER, M.C., and SHERMAN, W.L. (1979). "The Course of Mexican History." New York: Oxford University Press.

NAVA, J. (1969). "Mexican Americans; Past, Present, and Future." New York: American Book Company.

NAVA, J. (1973). "Viva La Raza!" New York: D. Van Nostrand.

NIMMO, D. and COMBS, J.E. (1980). "Subliminal Politics." Englewood Cliffs, NJ: Prentice-Hall.

PAZ, O, (1961). "The Labyrinth of Solitude." Trans. by L Kemp. New York: Grove Press.

PROSSER, M.H. (1978). "The Cultural Dialogue." Boston, MA: Houghton Mifflin.

ROSE, B. (1979). Risks in the tomato fields. *Toledo Blade* (29 July), (Sec. C), 1-3.

SHOB, D.E. (1975). "Hired Hands and Plowboys." Urbana, IL: University of Illinois Press.

SHOVER, J.L. (1976). "First Majority—Last Minority." DeKalb, IL: North-western Illinois University Press.

Strike prompts harassment by growers. (1979) *Nuestra Lucha 2* (Jan.), 1.

VELASQUEZ, B. (1979). (Keynote address to FLOC delegates, Aug. 4, Holgate, Ohio.)

VELASQUEZ, B. (1980). (Speech at Ohio State University, Jan. 23, Columbus, Ohio.)

PART II

COMMUNICATION INTERACTION

6

The "Faux Pas" in Interpersonal Communication

THOMAS E. HARRIS
University of Evansville
Evansville, Indiana 47702

Committing a "faux pas" appears to be a uniquely human experience. These social errors are frequently classified as bloopers or gaffes, or one may be thought to suffer from a case of "foot in mouth disease." After the commission, the relative positions of the actors in the interaction become strongly reaffirmed, and the occurance is treated with various social strategies ranging from laughter, which may be used at the perpetrator's expense, to the use of laughter by the perpetrator to indicate embarrassment. In the end the incident may be ignored, dealt with with a simple "oops!", or covered up altogether.

All of these contingencies surface in the classic children's tale of "The Emperor's New Clothes," (Anderson, 1958). The young boy lacked the social grace to label the Emperor's new clothes, which were non-existent, as attractive, since he was not schooled or privy to the requirements of society that the Emperor's opinions and position be reaffirmed. By pointing out loudly that the Emperor was naked, the boy comitted a blunder in manners and conduct, which is the definition of a "faux pas" forwarded by most dictionaries (Klein, 1966 vol. 1, p. 578).

Although the origin of the term "faux pas," which literally means a false step (Brewer, 1963, p. 354), is unclear, it can be traced back at least as far as the 17th Century. *The Oxford English Dictionary* (1983, vol. 4, p. 107) calls it "an act which compromises one's reputation, especially a woman's lapse from virtue." The analogy between a social blunder and a woman's loss of virtue indicates the impact these acts can have on interpersonal communication.

The origin of the word or the exact definition is probably unimportant, for few of us have difficulty in spotting a "faux pas," whether we actually cause it or are part of the audience that perceives it. In fact, the story of the Emperor's new clothes indicates the difficulty experienced when the audience is forced to try and cover up someone else's blunder. At one time or another, everyone has been made aware of the effect of their own false steps. The "faux pas" is largely non-discriminatory and has no apparent occupational boundaries, since it can occur in groups as diverse as politicians or classmates.

Although the "faux pas" is an easily labeled phenomenon, no systematic scheme has been presented for recognizing its characteristics. Various perspectives on the "faux pas" are available. Erving Goffman (1959, pp. 209-210), sees them as disruptions of the individual's projected image.

> Following common usage, such disruptions may be called "faux pas." Where a performer unthinkingly makes an intentional contribution which destroy's his team's image we may speak of "gaffes" or "boners." Where a performer jeopardizes the image of self projected by the other team, we may speak of "bricks" or of the performer having "put his foot in it."

He continues with the dramatistic analogy by stating:

> Unmeant gestures, inopportune intrusions, and "faux pas" are sources of embarrassment and dissonance which are typically unintended by the person who is responsible for making them and which would be avoided were the individual to know in advance the consequences of his activity.

The "faux pas," then, is acting out of place or incorrectly.

Examples of this particular interpersonal communication behavior are available from many sources. A recent article in *The New York Times* on college placement interviews related the following story.

> At the beginning of his college interview, the young man seemed earnest, a bit tense, eager to put his best foot forward. "What factors," I asked him, "influenced your consideration of colleges?"
>
> "Well . . . uh . . . to begin with, size is important to me. I don't want a huge college or a real small one; I want a mediocre college like Lafayette."
>
> I pretended not to notice his gaffe, and I doubt the young man realizes yet what he said. After all, some of the mistakes made by college applicants are unintentional, do not harm, and can be chalked up to nervousness and be quickly excused. The young man's word was amusing and not really damaging (Haines, 1980).

Cartoonists frequently use the "faux pas" for humor. Gary Trudeau (1976, p. 148), for example, in *Tales from the Margaret Mead Taproom*, has his famous character Duke from the Doonesbury comic strip acting as the governor of an island. A visitor from Washington, D.C. starts a conversation with Duke.

> Visitor: "Governor, there's a great story circulating in Washington!—They say you've been sacrificing virgins to the local volcano gods!"

No response from the governor.
Visitor: "Honestly! Isn't that just marvelous!? Ha, Ha, Ha, Ha! Ha, Ha!"
No response from the governor.
Visitor: "Heh . . ."
Duke: "Are you mocking my religious convictions?!"
Visitor: "Oh . . . No! I was just wondering!"

These slips of the tongue respect no national boundary and can have a bizarre political twist. At a royal luncheon in Glasgow, businessman Peter Balfour turned to the just-engaged Prince Charles and wished him a long life and conjugal happiness with Lady Jane. The attempt to be a well wisher was damaged by the dual "faux pas" presented by the facts that the Prince's wife to be was Lady Diana and that Lady Jane was one of the Prince's former flames (Rosenblatt, 1981).

William Safire (1978, p. 62), in *Safire's Political Dictionary*, labels such political acts as bloopers, which he defines as:

> an exploitable mistake; a slip of the tongue, or unthinking comment, that can be seized upon by the opposition. A "blooper" is worse than a "goof," more adult than a "boo-boo," not as serious as a "blunder," equivalent to a "gaffe." Repeated commission of any results in a description of having "foot-in-mouth disease."

France's Prime Minister Raymond Barre, for example, described the October 1980 bombing of a Paris synagogue as "this odious attack that was aimed at Jews and struck innocent Frenchmen" (Rosenblatt, 1981). His opponents quickly pointed out that the statement meant that Jews were neither innocent nor French and it also suggested that the attack would have been less odious had it been more selective and limited.

Kermit Schafer was able to amass a fortune from records and books, such as *Prize Bloopers*, which present many examples of such errors committed over the air. Art Linkletter (1967), in *Oops! Or, Life's Awful Moments*, has collected hundred of errors that he and other people have made.

As this introduction indicates, the "faux pas" is a distinctly human activity which requires interpersonal participation and evaluation. However, except for anecdotes and homely illustrations, we do not possess a theory of the "faux pas." This study suggests four characteristics of the "faux pas."

The first step in formulating the theory is to view these interpersonal interactions as rituals or presentations. From this perspective, the need to be dramaturgically aware and astute obviously exists. Goffman (1959, p. 216) warns that an effective participant is a "performer, dramaturgically speaking, [who] does not commit 'faux pas.' " The impact on the presentation is further explained:

> But, while a "gaffe" or "faux pas" can mean that a single individual is at one and the same time the cause of the incident, the one who feels embarrassed

by it, and the one for whom he feels embarrassment, this is not, perhaps, the typical case, for in these matters ego boundaries seem especially weak. When an individual finds himself in a situation which ought to make him blush, other present usually will blush with and for him, though he may not have sufficient sense of shame or appreciation of the circumstances to blush on his own account (Goffman, 1967, pp. 99-100).

Other terms provided from this perspective are useful. The actors in the ritual are expected to deliver the appropriate lines to maintain face. To maintain face, the individual in interpersonal communication must be internally consistent. As such, one must strive not to discredit the performance, which requires that one maintain his/her own face and the face of the other participants.

Goffman (1967, p. 12) concludes: "Ordinarily, maintenance of face is a condition of interaction, not its objective." This face maintenance is the capacity for "tact, 'savoir-faire,' diplomacy, or social skill" (Goffman, 1967, p. 13).

One must remember, however, that saving face is an interpersonal skill and phenomenon. "If a person is to employ his repertoire of face-saving practices, obviously he must first become aware of the interpretations he must place on them" (Goffman, 1967, p. 13). When the face or front is threatened because the actor has failed to avoid offensive consequences, these acts are called "faux pas, gaffes, boners, or bricks."

The perspective provided by Goffman gives the observer, or, for that matter, the active participant, the tools necessary to analyze the phenomena. What is needed is a systematic theory which explains the characteristics beyond the assumption that one can "be in the wrong place or say the wrong thing at the wrong time."

The first principle of the "faux pas" is that *it must be audienced.* One cannot commit an intrapersonal "faux pas." In fact, if the activity carries all the potential described by Goffman, but is not audienced, then a sigh of relief is probably the only response that will occur. The issue, then, is to avoid losing face or to maintain the quality of one's own presentation and composure in front of an audience.

The extent of the audiencing can be determined by asking three questions as stated by Goffman (1967, p. 99). "*By* whom is the embarrassing incident caused? *To* whom is it embarrassing? *For* whom is this embarrassment felt? It is not always an individual for whose plight participants feel embarrassment." In some manner, these questions must be asked, for regardless of the incident, the "faux pas" must be called to the attention of someone else, or the potential must exist that it will be called to someone else's attention. So, it can be explained and examined only as an interpersonal concept.

When we are involved in an interpersonal interaction, we try to maintain a sense of poise which indicates that we have retained our own composure. In most social interaction, the goal is to be gracious, to have tact, or to demonstrate social skill. So, embarrassment generated by a "faux pas" affects poise, which

> plays an important role in communication, for it guarantees that those present will not fail to play their parts in interaction but will continue as long as they are in one another's presence to receive and transmit disciplined communications (Goffman, 1967, pp. 103-104).

The concept of social poise is demonstrated by many youngsters when they resist "losing it" in various games and activities. The practical joke, to a large extent, requires the victim to fail to maintain composure. The ability to receive, symbolically, a "pie in the face" with grace is important for a socially aware individual.

The "faux pas," then, is the failure to respond in a gracious manner, to demonstrate a lack of social skill, or to threaten the audience with the potential that one will not be able to handle the interaction, and therefore bring about a loss of face.

"During interaction, the individual is expected to possess certain attributes, capacities, and information, which, taken together, fit into a self that is at once coherently unified and appropriate for the occassion" (Goffman, 1967, p. 105). None of these characteristics have any consequence, of course, unless the individual's attempts to interact effectively are audienced.

The second characteristic of the "faux pas" is that *it always involves an attempt to ingratiate*. When one feels the need to act in a manner that is appropriate to an unaccustomed situation, the potential for error is heightened. Every interpersonal interaction can be labeled as complementary or symmetrical for all the participants (Watlzawick et al., 1967, pp. 67-70). Persons committing social blunders seem to be in the process of attempting to ingratiate themselves. The attempt to come across as smooth and polished, in order to impress someone who is in a role that is perceived as complementary to one's own, can lead to difficulties. "There are many classic circumstances under which the self projected by an individual may be discredited, causing him shame and embarrassment over what he has or appears to have done to himself and the interaction" (Goffman, 1967, p. 107). This discrediting seems to occur when someone is speaking up to the other participants. Goffman (1967, p. 107) explains the problem. "To affect the style of one's occupational or social betters is to make claims that may be discredited by one's lack of familiarity with the role."

Since interpersonal interactions involve the agreed upon relationships between individuals, if both participants are unaware or fail to present the requisite skills for interaction, gaffes can occur. When one meets someone new and is concerned with "putting the best foot forward," errors can occur if there is a lack of sophistication in adapting one's role behavior. "Embarrassment, then, leads us to the matter of 'role segregation.' Each individual has more than one role, but he is saved from role dilemma by 'audience segregation' " (Goffman, 1967, p. 22). Goffman's concept of role safety through audience segregation is not possible to the degree that one is meeting new audiences. When one faces new audiences, the potential for error is increased, since the participant may not have the necessary skills for the new scene or audience. To the degree that actors feels the need to ingratiate themselves with the new audience, the interaction becomes complementary. The extra effort and importance placed on the interaction enhances the potential for a "faux pas."

The third rule of the "faux pas" follows logically. *The potential* for a "faux pas" *is inversely related to the amount of intimacy.* If the audience is well known, then the participant's means of dealing with the audience are also well known, and the likelihood of a "faux pas" is decreased. When the audience consists of close friends or the situation is familiar, the possibilities for blunders are reduced.

However, to the degree that the audience is changed, reconstituted by adding a new or unexpected element, or the reason for the gathering is varied, the potential for error increases since the intimacy of the occasion has changed. Since the initial social ritual of meeting someone or something new also involves some type of assessment of the person or situation, errors are more likely to be noted. Newcomers provide a focus for the participants that has greater impact than the ongoing interaction. The likelihood of a "faux pas" in the middle of an intimate conversation certainly does not disappear completely, but the potential would seem to decrease. Most persons can recall the error of muttering an old lover's name at the wrong time, but the majority of social blunders occur when it is difficult to label them as stupid or simply indiscreet.

An interesting addition to this concept is that the audience also tends to be embarrassed over someone's embarrassment. In an intimate situation, this is not a particularly serious issue, since the relationship has already sustained difficult times. The spiraling effect in a non-intimate situation may work to the benefit of the person who created the problem. To the degree that the person indicates the appropriate amount of embarrassment over the blunder, the audience may actually give credibility to the person and shore up the individual. The audience's response, however, may be so overwhelming that it makes it difficult for the individual to remove him/herself from the error. The effect may be to heighten the "faux pas" so that it cannot be dismissed. The ultimate irony is that the audience's attempt to forgive the person and revalidate the social situation may actually lead to a form of exclusion. This is especially true if the audience expects some particular type of chagrin from the person, and it is not forthcoming. In that case, one may appear insensitive for not giving the reasonable response in the form of embarrassment.

In either case, the act is given attention and therefore must be acted upon. The responsible person may eventually gain by having the audience come to his/her assistance, or lose by not acting out the role of embarrassment properly. In any case, the desire on the part of the participants to have the initial stages of the interaction go smoothly enhances the likelihood of a "faux pas."

The final characteristic of the "faux pas" is that *it can only be forgiven by the other party or audience.* To the degree that the error has been audienced, one cannot simply ignore the "faux pas" in the hope that it will disappear. One is truly trapped in an interpersonal communication bind in which the other persons must communicate some type of release before the error can go away. Being "let off the hook" is important, however, for one's front or face has been threatened. Goffman (1967, p. 22) describes certain actions that can be taken.

> The phases of the corrective process—challenge, offering, acceptance, and thanks—provide a model for interpersonal ritual behavior, but a model that may be departed from in significant ways. For example, the offended parties may give the offender a chance to initiate the offering on his own before a challenge is made and before they ratify the offense as an incident. This is a common courtesy, extended on the assumption that the recipient will introduce a self-challenge. Further, when the offended persons accept the corrective offering, the offender may suspect that this has been grudgingly done from tact, and so he may volunteer additional corrective offerings, not allowing the matter to rest until he has received a second or third acceptance of his repeated apology. Or the offended persons may tactfully take over the role of the offender and volunteer excuses for him that will, perforce, be acceptable to the offended persons.

All of the recovery techniques, however, require that the audience practice forgiveness.

There are, of course, various types of incidents. "When a minor mishap occurs, momentarily revealing a person in wrong face or out of face, the others are often more willing and able to act blind to the discrepancy than is the threatened person himself." (Goffman, 1967, p. 28). So, given all the options, the audience will choose to disregard some incidents.

The audience is not always able to forgive easily or to ignore the blunder, since the level of intimacy is not high and the audience cannot be certain of the perpetrator's next move.

> Thus, when a person makes a slight "gaffe," he and the others may become embarrassed not because of an inability to handle such difficulties, but because for a moment no one knows whether the offender is going to act blind to the

incident, or give it joking recognition, or employ some other face-saving practice (Goffman, 1967, p. 27).

In addition, the audience may not know who has been threatened in the interaction. "Terms such as 'gaffe' or 'faux pas' fail to specify whether it is the actor's own face he has threatened or the face of other participants." (Goffman, 1967, p. 28).

However, when the interpersonal communication process has been affronted by a "faux pas," only the other participants in the process can act to save the event. "Interestingly enough, when the person commits a 'gaffe' against himself, it is not he who has the license to forgive the event; only the others have that prerogative" (Goffman, 1967, p. 33).

Actually, there are many tools available to the person to receive forgiveness. "Explanations, apologies, and joking are all ways in which the individual makes a plea for disqualifying some of the expressive features of the situation as sources of definition of himself." (Goffman 1961, p. 105). As long as the audience agrees to accept these as releases, the interaction will continue. If the audience refuses to forgive, then the error takes on even greater significance.

These four characteristics of the "faux pas" emerge from the perspective provided by seeing interactions as social performances. The "faux pas" must be audienced, it always involves an attempt to ingratiate, it is inversely related to the amount of intimacy, and it can only be forgiven by the other party or audience.

The study of interpersonal communication involves the understanding of interactions between individuals where some rules of behavior are followed. Successful interpersonal behavior requires some ability to adapt and follow these rules of behavior. The "gaffe" or "faux pas" is the antithesis of role behavior. It is useful to return to Goffman (1967, p. 51), who observes:

> An act that is subject to a rule of conduct is, then, a communication, for it represents a way in which selves are confirmed—both the self for which the rule is an obligation and the self for which it is an exception. An act that is subject to rules of conduct but does not conform to them is also communication—often even more so—for infractions make news and often in such a way as to disconfirm the selves of the participants. Thus rules of conduct transform both action and inaction into expression, and whether the individual abides by the rules or breaks them, something significant is likely to be communicated.

With no difficulty, the "faux pas" fits into this definition of communication. In addition, it cannot exist without interpersonal communication behavior. Mark Twain once observed, "Man is the only animal that blushes. Or needs to." That statement, of course, returns to the initial observation that the "faux pas" occurs all around us. With the four principles provided by this study, perhaps we can go further than simply observing that people do indeed blush and get embarrassed.

REFERENCES

ANDERSEN, H.C. (1958). The emperor's new clothes. *In* N. Beust (Ed.), "Fun and Fantasy." Eau Claire, WI: E. M. Hale and Company.

BREWER E.C. (1963). "Brewer's Dictionary of Phase & Fable." London: Cassell.

GOFFMAN, E. (1959). "The Presentation of Self in Everyday Life." Garden City, New York: Doubleday.

GOFFMAN, E. (1961). "Encounters: Two Studies in the Sociology of Interaction." Indianapolis, IN: Bobbs-Merrill.

GOFFMAN, E. (1967). "Interaction Ritual: Essays on Face-to-Face Behavior." Chicago, IL: Aldine.

HAINES, R.W. (1980). Interviewing. *New York Times* (Nov. 16), E 1.

KLEIN, E. (1966). "A Comprehensive Etymological Dictionary of the English Language." Amsterdam, Holland: Elsevier Publishing Co.

LINKLETTER, A. (1967). "Oops! or, Life's Awful Moments." Garden City, New York: Doubleday.

"Oxford English Dictionary." (1933). Oxford, England: Clarendon Press.

ROSENBLATT, R. (1981). Oops! How's that again? *Time* (March 30), 85.

SAFIRE, W. (1978). "Safire's Political Dictionary." New York: Ballantine Books.

TRUDEAU, G.B. (1976). "Tales from the Margaret Mead Taproom." Kansas City, MO: Andrews and McMeel.

WATLZAWICK, P., BEAVIN, J.H., and JACKSON, D.D. (1967). "Pragmatics of Human Communication." New York: W.W. Norton.

7

Communicational Aspects of Status Transition

JANET FARRELL
University of Pennsylvania
Philadelphia, Pennsylvania 19104

When I was in the 4th grade, my best friend showed up at my door one day wearing nylon stockings instead of the customary knee socks. My explanation for her change in attire rested in my understanding that girls could wear nylons when they stopped getting scabs on their knees. I couldn't wear them yet, I thought, because my knees were obviously scraped and skinned and nylon stockings wouldn't hide the bruises as knee socks would. This explanation sufficed for the time being.

Whether the young girl shifts from knee socks to nylons or the young boy from short pants to longer ones, the transition to adulthood in any society involves progression through an age-graded system of appropriate behavior. This paper is concerned with the "informal" markers of "coming of age" in our society; that is, the culturally available means for marking junctures between age-grades. Status transition is discussed from the perspective of the life cycle. The transition from the "asexual" world of childhood to social puberty or adolescence is examined as a communicational problem.

The learning of sex membership is, of course, a lifelong process, as Mead (1949) has noted. We do not suddenly emerge from a chrysalis to be dramatically christened with sexuality at, say, age 13. Rather, we constantly experience "maleness" and "femaleness" in our relations with others, and, depending on our individual temperaments, adapt to this exposure in various ways. Listening to the ticking of our "social clocks," however, there is an intensification of concern with preparations for adult genitality at some phase of the life cycle. This phase is referred to here as social puberty or adolescence.

Van Gennep's (1960) work on "rites de passage"[1] examined the cere-

---

[1]Van Gennep developed the following schema to characterize the transition from one defined social position to another: rites of separation, transition rites, and rites of incorporation. Besides life cycle transitions, Van Gennep also discussed territorial passage.

monies through which an individual passes on all of the most important occasions in his or her life. The "rites of passage" take many forms and occur at various points in the life cycle, such as birth, childhood, social puberty, marriage, and death. The class of events marking entrance into social puberty is referred to as "initiation rites." In performing these rites, boys and girls are incorporated into the adult society of the sexes. According to Van Gennep (1960, p. 67):

> These are rites of separation from the asexual world, and they are followed by rites of incorporation into the world of sexuality and, in all societies and all social groups, into a group confined to persons of one sex or another.

Although initiation rites tend to take cermonial form in "primitive" societies (such as clitoral excision, public defloration, circumcision, physical isolation, or dietary taboos), there are only a few occasions in contemporary American society that might be comparable (for example, sweet 16 parties or bar/bas mitzvahs). For the most part, entrance into sex membership in our society is a gradual and informal process that relies on "customary" ritual.[2] That is, while "formal" ritual is used here to refer to ceremonial behavior, "customary" ritual denotes everyday behavior that is equally patterned and predictable.

Benedict (1938) considered contrasted sex roles to be the major discontinuity in the life cycle. Eventually, if the society is to perpetuate itself, the son or daughter must become a mother or father. The socially scripted behavior for the young boy or girl must change at some point. When the youth enters into sex membership at social puberty, gender-identification becomes more salient.

Gender-identification refers here to the use of artifactual and behavioral markers of masculinity and femininity. In that these markers are age-graded, they may also be called maturational markers. Gender-identification for females, for example, may involve the use of clothing, makeup, and hairstyling, as well as other events. Birdwhistell (1964) distinguished three types of sexual characteristics operating in gender-identification and response: primary, secondary, and tertiary. Clothing and cosmetological devices are classed as "tertiary," in that they are learned and situationally produced.

Gender-identification may be thought of as social communicational, in Birdwhistell's (1952) sense of integrational communication,[3] when approached from the standpoint of the positional marking of an age-sex category. As a taxonomic device, age-sex categories serve as links for social-structural

---

[2] As noted by Leach (1968).

[3] "Integrational" communication involves such interaction as invokes common past experience and is related to the initiation, maintenance, or severance of interaction (Birdwhistell, 1952, pp. 3-4).

continuity.[4] Members within each age-sex category are equipped with patterns for reciprocal behavior with members of other age-sex groups within the society. When individual persons enter into the patterned behavior appropriate for their age and sex, the organizational scheme of a society is reconfirmed.

The investigation of gender-identification as social communication discussed here is exploratory in nature, focusing on the nature and timing of age-graded markers for females only. I conducted 50 tape-recorded interviews at my former high school in suburban Philadelphia with two groups of girls who were following different social trajectories.[5] One group of girls planned to go to college after graduating from high school, and the other group decided to enter the working world. The interviewees were asked when they became interested in clothing, makeup, boys, and other orders of gender-related behavior. These self-reports were then analyzed with attention to the differences between the two groups.

Within this adolescent age grade,[6] evidence was found for the existence of consistent maturational markers. The transition from elementary school to junior high emerged as a juncture of great importance for both groups of girls. For example, during this time, a shift in attitude toward clothing was reported. According to one of the college-bound students:

> If you wore something weird to school, that was it, you were labeled . . . [I] used to have a pair of pants with horses on it, and you don't wear those things, [it's] weird.

Another states:

> It used to be a real fight for my mother to get me to go shopping for clothes, cause I hated it. I hated trying them on, and just about then [7/8th grade] I started to like it and want more clothes.

One of the interviewees noticed the change in her cousin's behavior:

> I've noticed like my cousin, she's almost 12, in the past couple years she's changed dressing. Before she would throw on anything, no matter what it looked like. Now she's more selective and she usually copies whatever I wear.

The attitude toward clothing was markedly different before junior high school, as one girl describes:

---

[4] As both Linton (1940) and Parsons (1942) have noted.

[5] By "social trajectory" I mean the path carved by an individual through the social system, or cumulative status changes made over the life cycle. It is a temporal pattern of social activity or behavior.

[6] Radcliffe-Brown (1929, p. 21) has defined "age grade" as "recognized divisions in the life of an individual as he passes from infancy to old age." In American society, these divisions are not as formal or rigid as commonly recognized in African societies, for example.

> I just remember how stupid I thought it was to get clothes for a present. I thought it was the stupidest thing on earth. I couldn't understand why my mom gave it to me, why I should be happy . . . If she bought you a bathrobe, I thought, you can go out and buy a bathrobe anytime, why should I waste a present?

The first bra emerged anywhere from 5th to 8th grade. The work-bound girls reported receiving their first bras somewhat earlier that their college-bound counterparts. One of the college-bound girls who received hers in the 8th grade reported:

> I can remember everyone else around me was getting them . . . the change from elementary school to junior high, you felt like you were growing up and you wanted one.

Cosmetological devices, such as makeup and perfume, were employed in stages. In the earlier phase of makeup usage, wearers were often excessive with its application. Not until an older sister or a girlfriend taught the young girl how to use the makeup did she then tone it down and make it look more "natural." This inability to use the makeup marker properly called attention to the youth of the user, as one interviewee claimed:

> My sister and her friends, wearing makeup and stuff, it just seems kind of funny to me that they're wearing makeup, they don't look like they should be . . . it just makes them look even younger.

Perfume usage also occurred in stages. When the interviewees were at a younger age, they reportedly preferred sweet and flowery scents. Come junior or senior high, however, more "sophisticated" brands were preferred. That certain scents are appropriate at certain ages was borne out by the testimony of one of the eleventh grade work-bound girls. She had just given her "Love's Baby Soft" (a sweet-smelling scent) to her younger sister.

Dating also progressed in stages which I have labeled: school romance, group dating, and coupling. In a school romance, a boy and a girl are putatively "going out" with one another, although they do not see each other outside of the school setting. With group dating, boys and girls will go out on a date *en masse*. There needn't be any particular pairing of members within the group. Finally, when heterosexual interest is manifested in individual initiative, that is, when a boy asks a girl out or vice versa, dating takes the form of coupling. "Having a boyfriend" becomes a behavioral maturational marker. One of the college-bound students described herself in the 9th grade:

> I wasn't interested in boys physically, I just wanted a boyfriend. I wanted a date for the dance but I really didn't know why I wanted them.

A variety of behavior shifts that more or less "closed" the "asexual" stage were discerned. Younger girls were seen as behaving differently towards boys than the interviewees themselves. Thinking back on how she used to relate to boys when she was younger, one of the girls reported:

> Like with boys, we'd always talk to them through another girlfriend or something, or through another friend. I don't think it was that we were shy, it's just that, that's the way we did it.

Another work-bound interviewee described the younger phase as:

> girls calling each other names and stealing each others boyfriends . . . [you] can't trust them, and the rumors go around and the gossip goes around.

Also, the appropriate time for sexual intercourse was thought to be in college, as opposed to high school:

> in college it's a different story. I couldn't see in high school. There's so much more to do with yourself . . . [your] chances of getting married to someone you're going out with in college is definitely better than in high school.

Besides these boy-related behavioral shifts, other changes occurred. For instance, there came a time when the young girls asserted control over the styling of their hair. Prior to this time, hair care and style were part of the mother's domain. Telephone usage also rose and declined in importance between 5th and 9th grade.

Although the somatic changes of the adolescent girl may act as gender cues, their role as markers is either enhanced or diminished by cross-referencing social considerations. A number of important social factors influenced gender-identification: the presence of older sisters or sister surrogates, reference groups, media usage, parental rules about gender-related behavior, finances, going to Catholic versus public school, etc. In one instance, one of the college-bound girls reported that her early interest in dating was stifled by parental restraints. Her parents were Italian immigrants who placed a high priority on education, presumably in the interest of social mobility. When their daughter expressed a desire to date, the parents insisted that "school comes first." Often, they would say: "He has to go to school and you have to go to school." As a result, they did not allow their daughter to date.

The findings that I have presented here are a first cut in an attempt to examine gender-identification as social communication. In sum, evidence was found that these markers are age-graded and that they follow a social timetable, rather than a biological one. Rather than viewing gender-identification as individual need fulfillment (as Malinowski would posit), such behavior, I would argue, requires social structural, and as such, social communicational, explanation.

REFERENCES

BENEDICT, R. (1938). Continuities and discontinuities in cultural conditioning. *Psychiatry 1*, 161-167.

BIRDWHISTELL, R.L. (1952). "Introduction to Kinesics." (Photo-offset.) Foreign Service Institute. Louisville, KY: University of Louisville Press.

BIRDWHISTELL, R.L. (1964). "The Tertiary Sexual Characteristics of Man: A Fundamental in Human Communication." (Reprint.) Also published in his "Kinesics and Context." Philadelphia, PA: University of Pennsylvania Press, 1970.

LEACH, E.R. (1968). Ritual. *International Encyclopedia of the Social Sciences 13*, 520-526.

LINTON, R. (1940). A neglected aspect of social organization. *American Journal of Sociology 45*, 870-886.

MEAD, M. (1949) "Male and Female." New York: William Morrow & Co.

PARSONS, T. (1942). Age and sex in the social structure of the United States. *American Sociological Review 7*, 604-616.

RADCLIFFE-BROWN, A.R. (1929). Age organization terminology. *Man 29*, 21.

VAN GENNEP, A. (1960). "The Rites of Passage." Trans. by M. B. Vizedom and G. L. Chaffee. Chicago, IL: University of Chicago Press.

8

Eye Behavior of Men and Women When They Argue

JOHN ALFRED JONES
University of Illinois at Chicago Circle
Chicago, Illinois 60680

This research examines American use of eye and eyebrow involvement during argument. Specifically, eyebrow and eyelid motion are examined to determine whether or not distinctive differences emerge in such behavior to reflect varied intensity levels of disagreement. Also, the variable of gender will enter into the above issue.

Recent research has provided only related insight. For example, studies of pupillary activity have been extensive but not directed toward arguers. Representative studies include Barlow (1969), Ekman et al. (1980), Goleman (1981), Hays and Plax (1971), Hess (1975), Janisse and Peavler (1974), Knapp (1978), Morris (1977), and Woodmansee (1970). Similarly, extensive notational systems for coding facial motion have been developed, but have most frequently been applied under laboratory rather than field conditions (see Ekman et al., 1980; Hays and Plax, 1971; Hess, 1975; Janisse and Peavler, 1978).

PROCEDURE

Teams of three independent observers each were assigned to selected geographic areas of Chicago. (All areas of the city were represented.) Each team member was trained in relevant observational techniques emphasizing: (a), how to perform unobtrusive coding; and (b), how to classify the observations.

The eye behavior of two-person arguers in spontaneous and natural circumstances was recorded on an observation sheet (see Fig. 1). Data was collected on the intensity of the disagreement, the sex of the arguers, and

FIGURE 1. Analyzing Nonverbal Communication During Dyadic (Two Person)
          Disagreements

Record Sheet:
   1. Intensity of Observed Disagreement (Circle One):

   High   Medium   Low (or Mild)

   2. Sex of the Diagreement Discussants (Circle Two and Indicate which
      One Is Person #1 and which is Person #2):

      #1   #2   #1   #2
      Male   Male   Female   Female

   3. Nonverbal Eye Behavior and Eyebrow Behavior During Disagreement:

Eye Opening Samples—⬡ increased eye opening; ⊖ squinted; ⊗ blinked

   Person #1 ◯◯
   Person #2 ◯◯

Eyebrow Behavior Samples—⋀up into high point;⋁down;⌢up rounded

   Person #1⋀ both,⋀one,⋁ both,⋁ one, ⌢ both, ⌢ one
   Person #2⋀both,⋀one,⋁ both,⋁one, ⌢ both, ⌢ one

the eyelid opening and eyebrow behavior of the two discussants. This coding
instrument was a refined version of one used in a pilot study, and high
reliability among observers on all coded items was achieved. Only those
arguments the observers chanced upon were recorded for this study. Only
those two-person arguments for which all three independent observers recorded identical notations were employed in the final analysis of the data.
Therefore, each person's eye and eyebrow behavior treated as a single observation in this study, in fact, represents agreement of observations by three
observers.

RESULTS

This city-wide field investigation in Chicago of 224 men and women during
two-person arguments reveals significant differences in eye behavior and no
significant differences in eyebrow behavior. The data of 100 men and 124
women engaged in arguments was subjected to chi-square analyses to assess
differences.

   Comparison of eye behavior across men, regardless of the argument's
intensity reveals that increased eyelid opening is more likely to occur during
arguments than either squinting or blinking, and that squinting is more likely

to occur than blinking (P<.001). The data ratios suggest a frequency of twice as many instances of increased eyelid opening as squinting and twice as much squinting as blinking.

Comparing the eye behavior of all women, regardless of the argument's intensity reveals that squinting is slightly more likely to occur than increased eyelid opening and nearly twice as likely to occur as blinking (P<.05).

Thus, the eye behavior of men compared with women, regardless of intensity of disagreement, reveals that men are somewhat more likely to increase eyelid opening, while women are nearly twice as likely to squint and nearly twice as likely to blink (P<.05).

When the intensity of disagreement is not an issue, no significant differences arise with respect to the possible gender combinations of arguers, i.e., men × men, men × women, or women × women. However, when argument intensity is a variable, the data show that women are approximately six times as likely to increase eyelid opening during medium-intensity arguments than during those of high intensity, and are approximately twice as likely to increase eyelid opening during medium intensity arguments than during those of low intensity (P<.005). Also frequencies suggest that women arguing with women are more than twice as likely to squint during low intensity arguments as during medium intensity arguments, and better than ten times more likely than during high intensity arguments (P<.005). Finally, women arguing with women are slightly more than twice as likely to blink during low intensity than during medium intensity arguments and approximately five times as likely to do so during low intensity arguing as during high intensity arguing (P<.05). Similar comparisons of men across the intensity levels reveal no significant differences.

Analysis of eyebrow behaviors reveals no significant findings in any of the comparisons.

DISCUSSION

The findings of this study are restricted to the general categories of men and women in a large urban area of the United States. Additional research should investigate various sub-categories such as ethnic identities and levels of education.

Despite these shortcomings, the findings of the present study suggest that eyelid behavior during arguments varies between men and women. These variations seem most related to the intensity of the disagreement among women.

REFERENCES

BARLOW, J.D. (1969). Pupillary size as an index of preference in political candidates. *Perceptual and Motor Skills 28*, 587-590.

EKMAN, P., FRIESEN, W., and ANCOLI, S. (1980). Facial signs of emotional experience. *Journal of Personality and Social Psychology 39,* 1125-1134.

GOLEMAN, D. (1981). The 7,000 faces of Dr. Ekman. *Psychology Today 15* (Feb), 42-49.

HAYS, E.R., and PLAX, T.G. (1971). Pupillary response to supportive and aversive verbal messages. *Speech Monographs 38,* 316-320.

HESS, E.H. (1975). The role of pupil size in communication. *Scientific American* (Nov.), 110-112, 116-119.

JANISSE, M.P., and PEAVLER, W.S. (1974). Pupillary research today: Emotion in the eye. *Psychology Today 7,* 60-63.

KNAPP, M.L. (1978). "Nonverbal Communication in Human Interaction," 2nd ed. New York: Holt, Rinehart and Winston.

MORRIS, D. (1977). "Manwatching." New York: Harry N. Abrams.

WOODMANSEE, J.J. (1970). The pupil response as a measure of social attitudes. *In* G. F. Summers (Ed.), "Attitude Measurement." Chicago, IL: Rand McNally.

9

Medical Training in Interpersonal Communication and the Care of Children Who May Die[1]

JAMES E. MORRISS
Dowling College
Oakdale, New York 11769

Caring for a child with a life-threatening illness is probably one of the most difficult tasks a physician must face. While medical training may equip physicians with technical expertise, medical doctors may lack the knowledge and communication skills necessary for effectively dealing with the coexisting psychosocial problems.

During the past 50 years, the medical curriculum has focused primarily on "hard" technical knowledge in an effort to keep up with the constant flow of new information and research data. However, "Medical students have not been taught to listen or to deal with fear, emotional pain, human despair, and sorrow . . . yet these are as much present and part of their professional daily life . . . as the treatment plan and the latest scientific findings" (Seeland, 1977).

The central problems described in this paper are:

1. What do parents of children with life-threatening illness most frequently note as problematic in doctor-patient relationships?
2. What are the kinds of knowledge and skills that may aid physicians in the prevention or resolution of such problems?
3. How do resident physicians in pediatrics evaluate current medical training in interpersonal skills related to the care of patient-family units faced with life-threatening illnesses?

Answers to the first question were derived from in-depth interviews with parents, pediatric nurses, and senior physicians. Comparison of data

---

[1] This material is based on the author's dissertation, "Medical Training in Interpersonal Communication and the Care of Children Who May Die," New York University, 1980.

from these three perspectives helped shed light on the nature of the problems the parents had cited. More than 100 subjects from hospitals in the Greater New York Metropolitan Area participated in this part of the study.

The second question was also approached through interviews with the same groups of parents, pediatric nurses, and senior physicians.

Clearly, these portions of the study were not concerned with an objective analysis of interaction, but with the perceptions of interactants regarding what transpires in situations of this kind.

Many parents complained about inadequacy of information:

> When my daughter was being treated for leukemia, our doctor always talked with us, she talked and talked and talked, but she never really answered any of our questions. I don't think she thought much of the questions we asked. I always felt diminished when I spoke with her.

> I remember once when they were going to try a new procedure for which I had to sign a permission form. It said right on the form that you were to be given ample opportunity to ask questions. . . . but when I asked our doctor about the procedure she said, "Oh, you don't need to worry about that. It's just something new."

> Doctors are often not prepared to answer your questions or to refer you to someone else. I don't think they recognize the parent's emotional need to know. There should be booklets for you to read. . . . I had to go to the encyclopedia to look it up.

> I always felt, if the doctor had spent just a little more time and given us just a little more information, it would have lessened the anxiety.

In regard to the parents' role in the care of the child, one parent noted:

> The hospital made me feel disassociated from my child. They were carrying out the treatment and we were made to feel we couldn't really take part in it. There were times when I even felt I was in the way. The parents should really be an integral part of the team. We need to be encouraged by the physicians to be active participants.

In regard to counselling, one parent said:

> We needed guidance about how much to say to our child and how to conduct ourselves, but this information was not available to us at the hospital and we had to seek it elsewhere.

Another parent noted that:

> We were left to our own devices in dealing with the children. The doctor doesn't think of these things. He is not trained to do this. Someone should have advised us but no one did.

Many parents complained about the "rounds," the "wall of white coats":

> They could have called the child by his name instead of his disease. The name is on the chart, you know.

Some parents had positive things to say about the physicians' interactions with them and with their children. One parent recalled how a doctor stooped down to the child's level when talking with him.

> It worked like magic, she said, and it didn't take any more of the doctor's time.

Another parent remembered that, in the emergency room, one older physician had picked up the child and held him in his arms.

> I'll never forget that doctor, the parent said, he treated my son as if he were his own and he said that though they didn't know what was wrong that they would do everything that was in their power to find out. His words and actions made us feel very much at ease.

In all, the interviews with the parents pointed to six significant problems:

1. the manner in which disclosure of the diagnosis/prognosis was made
2. the lack of adequate counselling regarding communication with the child about his or her illness
3. inadequate information regarding the child's condition and treatment during the course of the illness
4. lack of coordination of team effort in providing comprehensive care for the patient-family unit
5. failure to include the patient-family unit as team members in the management of the illness
6. lack of support for the patient-family unit when the child is dying

Nurses and senior physicians were presented with the problems most frequently cited by the parents. The nurses, like the parents, appeared to believe that one of the underlying causes of the problems was the lack of emphasis given in medical training to non-medical aspects of disease management. However, many of the nurses indicated that many of the problems in the care of children with life-threatening illness, paticularly problems such as avoidance and lack of information, stemmed from the doctors' fear of failure. Nurse comments included:

> I think one of the causes is that doctors have been trained to save, to cure. They have not learned to accept dying as part of living and they haven't learned to cope with their own feelings about death. I think there have to be changes way back in medical school. I think doctors have to stop considering death as a defeat. They have to learn to deal with other aspects of care like helping a family face a crisis.

> Doctors become unrealistic. They don't know when to stop. Instead of saying "this looks bad" and then supporting the family and the patient through the crisis, I see them focusing on this count and on this drug . . . it's really sad

because the kid suffers because he gets scared, and all they really need is just someone to be there.

In dealing with cases like this, if the doctor hasn't come to grips with his own mortality he, in turn, sets up defenses. He appears aloof, disinterested, or impersonal in his relationships with the child or the family. An increase in formal education in death and dying would improve the doctors' ability to understand the feelings of others in these situations.

All the senior physicians interviewed were doctors with many years of experience in pediatric care. Most of them were professors of pediatrics, and a number were heads of pediatric departments at major cancer research institutions. A typical physician noted:

It's not easy for the physician when he sees the treatment protocol he has designed is not working or that the child is failing in spite of everything he is doing. There is a sense of failure that is very personal and deep. There is a little of the heroic in every doctor and he doesn't like to fail. We don't even understand why we are keeping the child alive by "heroics," but you have to understand the doctor's need to have success with treatment. It is difficult to tell the parents that there is nothing more that you can do. It is easier to continue with the "heroics."

One physician, who had been a patient herself, said that she believed that every doctor needed to have that experience before practicing medicine. "It changes your perspective," she said. She also noted:

The important thing for the doctor is to be in touch with his own feelings. He needs to know the source of his anger with his patients. If he has not resolved his fear with death, he will not be much support to his patients. This may even be the source of his anger. There is no question that medical schools can help point this out and can teach the needs of people.

Another senior physician commenting on medical school training said;

A doctor's training is reactive-type training. You have to pick out, from four possibilities, why. You have to reproduce and fit back in data and those data have to be sorted, corrective factors added. In other words, a good resident physician functions like a computer. There is not much opportunity for talk in medical shcool. When a young doctor is faced with a bereaved parent whose child is wired up to the hilt with tubes in and out, he'll be at a loss for words and will feverishly examine the charts in order to reproduce a couple of data he knows how to deal with.

A survey was developed to obtain opinions and recommendations of resident pediatric physicians regarding current medical training in each of the problem areas identified.

Out of 300 pediatric residents contacted in 14 hospitals in the Greater New York Metropolitan Area, over one-third responded. Of the doctors responding to the survey, 90% indicated that they had cared for children with life-threatening illness on 3 to 10 occasions and 84% indicated that they had been the child's primary physician on two or more of these occasions.

Responding physicians completed a written questionnaire composed of three sections. In the first section, each of the six problem areas noted earlier was represented by a statement regarding the adequacy of medical training, which was to be evaluated in terms of a five-point scale. Each of these statement was worded in "positive" form (i.e., indicating that medical training was at least sufficient), and thus, the responding physician would indicate the extent to which he/she agreed with that statement. For example:

> I believe that current medical training adequately prepares physicians for counselling families regarding a life-threatening diagnosis/prognosis.

Of the responding physicians, not one indicated strong agreement with any of the six "positive" statements. In short, the majority of respondents "disagreed" or "strongly disagreed" with the statements, and, thus, most physicians indicated the inadequacy of medical training in the six areas of importance.

In the second section, responding physicians were asked for more open-ended comments on the issues of concern.

With respect to the disclosure of a life-threatening diagnosis/prognosis, a typical respondant wrote:

> There is no training at all. You learn only when forced into the situation. If you're lucky you will see someone else doing it first before you have to do it yourself.

In response to the item regarding information about the patient's condition and treatment, one resident responded with the following comment:

> One of the worst clinical skills of the average physician is in explaining clearly to patients the who/why/where/when/how of their diseases.

In regard to providing support for the patient-family unit when the child is dying, one resident, from one of the nation's most prestigious medical centers, wrote:

> In the first few months, when there was still hope for recovery, over half of the house staff was attending the child and interacting with the child's family. Now, the child has been in the process of dying for the past two weeks, and I and the child's attending physician are the only members of the staff who will talk with the mother.

In the third section of the survey information was requested regarding the physician's training in 21 areas of interpersonal skills and courses in the psychosocial aspects of disease management which are now being offered in many medical schools (Kahn et al., 1979). Respondents indicated that they had received training in many of the interpersonal skills areas listed in the questionnaire, and some of them had taken courses dealing with the psychosocial aspects of disease management. The respondents' evaluation of these course offerings varied considerably, however. There was significant agreement among the young doctors responding to the survey regarding the need for earlier introduction of, and greater continuity in, course offerings in these areas. Many of them indicated that, instead of the "one shot" offerings, training in interpersonal skills and the psychosocial aspects of disease management should begin in pre-med and continue through internship and residency.

In an age of spectacular technological progress we have, perhaps, become overly optimistic about the ability of science to satisfy all our needs. In this consumer culture, we are bombarded daily with messages proclaiming quick technological solutions to problems. In this age of wonder drugs, heart transplants, and computer diagnoses, we may come to acknowledge what technology lacks.

As we look through the lens of life-threatening illness in children at the issues which become important to those who face a possible loss, we are made aware of the larger human dilemma and the need for interpersonal communication as an important therapy in the care of childern who may die.

REFERENCES

KAHN, G.S., COHEN, B., AND JASON, H. (1979). The teaching of interpersonal skills in U.S. medical schools. *Journal of Medical Education 54*, 29.

SEELAND, I. (1977). "Physician-Patient Communication Patterns in the Clinical Setting and the Implications for the Education of the Medical Student in Thanatology." (Paper delivered at Foundation of Thanatology Conference, Columbia Presbyterian Hospital, New York City, N.Y.)

PART III

COMMUNICATION AND IDEOLOGY

10

Ideology: Symbols and Functions

DAN F. HAHN
Queens College
Flushing, New York 11367

One of the most pervasive of the roles performed by ideology is reification, the process by which "human artifacts, including 'ideas,' are invested with a power and a reality that are supposedly independent both of their producers and of the material conditions and operations involved in their production" (Aiken, 1964, p. 32). The fact that people are ready to die for an ideology which has no objective referent can be traced to the process of reification.

Because ideology becomes reified, it loses contact with reality.

> the idea or abstract concept is accorded a degree of reality above that of the specific, tangible instance or event. Thus, "History," "Revolutions," "Proletariat," "Socialism," are more real and important in the Communist mind than are specific events, revolutions, workers, or socialist policies. When the general rule and the specific instance do not jibe, the specific instance is dismissed as defective or transitional; the prior is never questioned (Daniels, 1963, pp. 328-329).

Out of contact with reality, the ideology becomes a religion accepted on faith. The words which the ideologue uses to relate self to society no longer relate to reality—they become a litany which believers recite to each other and teach to their children. Ralph Ross (1957, p. 169) reports that a schoolteacher once overheard the following Pledge of Allegiance: "I pledge my legions to the flag, and the Republicans for which it stands; one nation invisible, with liberals and justice for all."

To say that ideology reverts to meaningless ritual is not to say that the ideology is necessarily false, but that it is accepted as true without any objective measurement of its truthfulness. In this respect, ideology functions as a frozen idea.

When the ideology ceases to be a ritual, when it becomes connected again with individual and social reality, then it is transformed from ideology into an idea. It is as if the ideology were a seed, resting for years in sand and than transplanted into fertile ground where it grows again. An ideology, then, is at the same time a deceptive *substitute* for an idea and its *preservation*, until the time has come for its revival (Fromm, 1961, p. 124).

The process of reification is the result of at least three separate "causes." First, it is caused by the initial need for simplification in an overly-complex world. Thus, the word "proletariat" becomes a simplification for "workers of the world." The word might, at first, relate specifically to certain beliefs about the fate of those workers, but it soon degenerates into an "emotional" word connoting general dissatisfaction with the world at large, workers or no workers. As Kenneth Burke (1950, p. 32) so rightly notes, the danger of this reification by simplification process is that "it is but a step from treating inanimate nature as mere 'things' to treating animals, and then enemy peoples, as mere things."

A second cause of reification is the seemingly natural desire of humans to believe in something, the impulse to faith. If an ideology initially makes sense to us, we put our faith in it, and from that point on assume that the ideology still makes sense in our world. But no static ideology can portray accurately an ever-changing world.

Third, reification is the result of a misunderstanding of the nature of language. Most people are not aware of the independence a symbol has from the thing symbolized. There are too many people who would agree with the little boy who said, "Pigs are called pigs because they are such dirty animals." Further, most societies encourage such "thinking" through something similar to Fourth of July speeches, whereby the speaker aligns both self and audience with all the "right" symbols. In short, reification makes possible a unity between peoples on the symbolic level, in approximately this fashion: "I believe in x, y, and z and am therefore a Communist; Mr. B says he is a Communist and therefore must believe in x, y, and z. Therefore, Mr. B is a compatriot of mine and we must join together to fight all non-Communists, i.e., non-believers." Ideological symbols weld people into society and plant the seeds of ethnocentrism.

A second function of ideology, closely related to reification, is its poetic or inspirational role. When reification has taken place, symbols have replaced the content of ideology. These symbols then help to achieve unification between peoples. But the use of symbols does more than unify; it reinforces the faith. Arguments convince, but symbols inspire. World War I was fought to "make the world safe for democracy" by many people who could not have begun to define "democracy." Millions of people salute stars and stripes or hammers and sickles without any knowledge of what each of those symbols represents. Believers are inspired by listening to a Roman Catholic priest recite an unintelligible Latin litany. The effect upon them is poetic or in-spirational. It is clear that policy can change without any corresponding change in the poetry. Just as many U.S. citizens in 1982 believe ardently in "The American Way" as did citizens in 1920, yet it is obvious that the "Way" is different in each case. Likewise, "the style and rhetoric of Marxist-Leninist utterance has not departed significantly from the Stalinist norm" (Kline, 1964, p. 177), although the policies of the U.S.S.R. today are certainly different from those carried out by Stalin.

A third personal function of ideology is simplification. Simplification can be either beneficial or harmful, but it is always necessary:

> simplification is an essential feature of any rational initiation of action. To refuse to simplify when one confronts a problem is in effect to reject the obligation to reach a solution; it is to make a game of possibilities and hence to move au-tomatically outside the context of agency and choice. Every procedure that helps us to make decisions does so precisely by reducing the range of possibilities which we may reasonably be expected to consider (Aiken, 1964, p. 38).

Thus, simplification can have beneficial aspects. The question remains, how-ever, as to the benefits of ideological simplification. The possibility of benefits is reduced by the prejudice inherent in ideological simplification. That is, rather than allowing the ideologue to examine any problem and reduce it to its inherent components, ideology presupposes knowledge of the problem before it arises and dictates the solution blindly. Prejudgement replaces objective examination. Solutions are not directed to the problems; rather, problems are redefined to fit the dictated solutions.

A fourth important function of ideology for the individual is to provide roles to play in society or, at the very least, justifications for the roles played. "Both the struggling small businessman rehearsing his boundless confidence in the inevitable justness of the American system and the neglected artist attributing his failure to his maintenance of decent standards in a Philistine world are able . . . to get on with their work" (Geertz, 1964, p. 55). Ideology creates some roles, legitimizes other, and provides rationalization for either success or failure in any role chosen.

A fifth function of ideology is self-deception, for "it is the very nature of ideology that it deceives not only others, but also those who use it" (Fromm, 1961, p. 130). The deception may be "beneficial," as when it rationalizes the role the individual plays in society or makes the role more palatable. It may also be "harmful," as when it leads to an incorrect analysis of a problem or prompts its adherents to disregard an existing problem completely.

The main roles ideology plays for the individual, then, are reification, poetry (thus inspiration), simplification of life, provision of roles, and self-deception. While some of these functions are essentially healthy, the total effect may be destruction of self and society if we delude ourselves into reacting ideologically rather than objectively. As Anatole France wrote, "To give one's life for a belief is a high price to pay for conjecture."

REFERENCES

AIKEN, H.D. (1964). The revolt against ideology. *Commentary 37* (April), 29-39.

BURKE, K. (1950). "A Rhetoric of Motives." New York: Prentice-Hall.

DANIELS, R.V. (1963). "The Nature of Communism." New York: Vintage Books.

FROMM, E. (1961). "May Man Prevail? An Inquiry into the Facts and Fictions of Foreign Policy." Garden City, NY: Doubleday Anchor.

GEERTZ, C. (1964). Ideology as a cultural system. *In* D. E. Apter (Ed.), "Ideology and Discontent." New York: Free Press.

KLINE, G.L. (1964). Philosophy, ideology, and policy in the Soviet Union. *Review of Politics* 26 174-190.

ROSS, R. (1957). "Symbols and Civilizations." New York: Harcourt, Brace and World.

11

Professional Ideology and the Politics of Cultural Defining

LESLIE RADO
Yale University
New Haven, Connecticut 06520

Recent studies of the politics of knowledge have collapsed the traditional distinction between knowledge, on the one hand, and ideology on the other. Knowledge and proper science once meant truth, invariable truth beyond human interest, and ideology meant something less: the study of ideas; motivated or "interested" ideas; secularized belief systems; or false consciousness (see Gouldner, 1976). With Marx, the concept of ideology emerged along with the insight that some kinds of knowledge are socially variable. Recently, some areas of social thought exhibit a curious reflexiveness which compresses the distance between consciousness and its determinants. The notions derived from Marx remain entertwined, but in rather different ways: Marcuse (1968, pp. 223-224), as well as Habermas (1970, 1971) draw the close cousin of science, technology, into the realm of ideology. Smith (1974, as quoted in Tuchman, 1978, p. 178) states:

> There is no other way to know than humanly and therefore the knower is situated historically and culturally. . . . If to be situated as such entails ideology (indeed, if to be human entails ideology), then knowledge [and science as knowledge] is fundamentally ideological.

The ideological nature of knowledge and science extends to the knower. Scientists, technocrats, and other professionals are, to some extent, ideologues (see Schudson, 1978, 1980; Tuchman 1978; Johnson, 1977). Professionals are socialized to a view of the world and of their position in it; they are members of a socially situated, "interested" class. And professional education at its best constitutes an expertise that claims cultural authority over an area of knowledge.

The concern of this essay, however, is not the professions in general as a class distinct from non-professionals, but is rather the conflict between two different professions' claims to control the definition of a complex, contemporary issue: the redefinition of death in terms of brain function. I will analyze the interpretations and motives of ethicists (moral philosophers and theologians) and physicians, as well as the "discourse" between them, in an effort to suggest some limited and tentative responses to two rather Gargantuan questions. In what ways does ideology characterize professional debate? How far into the grounds of knowledge and conceptualization does ideology extend? The discussion rests on an analysis of arguments made by 39 physicians and 15 ethicists regarding their cultural authority to define death and influence public policy. These arguments are drawn from professional journals (1965-1974), surveys, and interviews conducted in 1975-1976 (for more specific methodological detail, see Rado, 1979, 1981).

"BRAIN DEATH"

The notion that death could and should be redefined to include the absence of brain as well as cardio-respiratory function emerged in the mid-1950s, along with the use of respirator and resuscitation technologies. These technologies interrupted the usually integrated systemic functioning of the dying human body by assuming the functions of the lungs and heart after the brain had stopped functioning. Still another medical technology, organ transplantation, prompted the reconceptualization of the locus and meaning of death. Two primary and profound problems emerged along with technological advances: (a), the presence of "unburied corpses"—"persons" whose hearts appeared to beat naturally, but whose brains had died; and (b), the demand for well-oxygenated organs for transplantation, especially the heart. Redefining death was proposed as a solution.

A quiet, yet profound, instance of cultural change, redefining death has entailed the reexamination of the ground, existential meanings of life and personhood. A state once determinable by most of us in fact, if not customary practice, now, at times, demands a special neurological skill and technique. The heart, long the seat of emotion and personality, not to mention life, has been reduced to a "replaceable muscle" (Paul Ramsey's phrase, 1970).

Physicians led the redefining effort until 1968, when ethicists entered the arena, most often to voice opposition to the medical consensus. Their separate purposes and interpretations fashion a sharp contrast. In many ways their debate fits the traditional conflict between moral and technological reason.

THE INTERPRETATIONS

Three conceptually integral indices of their respective positions are examined specifically: (a), reasons for redefining death; (b), characterization of the issue in terms of appropriate competency for managing it; and (c), concerns most frequently raised in the articles.

Rationale

In Table 1, we see that most physicians chose a primarily utilitarian rationale for defining death, arguing that the redefinition would serve certain purposes: facilitating organ transplantation and allowing the cessation of futile medical treatment.

> Insofar as transplantation of organs is facilitated [(by redefining death)] death may even be viewed as a creative act, in the sense that another desperately ill individual may be made whole by the gift of an organ. (Luchi, 1971, p. 284)

> It is extraordinarily expensive both financially and emotionally to maintain a dead person on a respirator in an intensive care unit or anywhere else, for an indefinite period. (Corbett, 1974, p. 86)

Both ethicists and physicians thought redefining death would reestablish an ethic of allowing persons to die humanely.

> The concept of "cerebral death" as a substitute for the cessation of heart beat and respirations as a definition of death appeals to many interested in the quality of life rather than mere existence. (Lowrey, 1971, p. 257)

The distinction between "ceasing futile treatment" and "allowing to die" is slippery under the best of circumstances. The two reasons were distinguished in terms of whether the rationale was oriented toward the "common good"— the benefit of family, other patients or the community at large—or toward the dying patient. Few ethicists agreed with physicians that death should be redefined to obtain organs, and most questioned the entire effort to

TABLE 1   Rationale

Death should be redefined in order to:	Medicine N = 39	Ethics N = 15
1. facilitate general transplantation	64.1 (25)	20.0 (3)
2. cease useless, futile prolongation of life	66.7 (26)	26.7 (4)
3. allow persons to die humanely	46.2 (18)	33.3 (5)
4. redefinition is not needed, or redefinition presents serious problems	9.7 (3)	73.3 (11)

redefine death, arguing that it was fraught with serious ethical and philosophical difficulty.

> We do not know with certainty the borderline between life and death, and a
> definition cannot substitute for knowledge. . . . In this state of marginal ig-
> norance and doubt, the only course to take is to lean over backward toward the
> side of possible life. (Jonas, 1974, p. 138)

What Kind of Issue is Redefining Death?

Authors made statements identifying the definition of death as a specific kind
of issue, statements which implicitly link the topic with a particular expertise,
either: (a), professional or non-professional "expertise"; or (b), among the
professions, legal, medical, or philosophical/ethical expertise (see Table 2).
Most statements distinguished between the determination or declaration of
death, and the definition of death, the first referring to the practices and
criteria utilized to assess death, the second to the concept and meanings to
which those practices and criteria ultimately refer. About half of the physicians indicated that both were medical matters. Those who stated that the
definition required other kinds of competencies most often mentioned legal
competencies; in this process most lawyers functioned to formally confirm
medical opinion. Unlike the ethicists, few physicians, considered this a matter
of lay concern or public determination.

> The *basic concept* of death is fundamentally a philosophical matter. . . . In
> setting forth the *general physiological standard(s)* for recognizing death, the

TABLE 2   What kind of issue is redefining death?

	Medicine $N = 39$	*Ethics* $N = 15$
1. Determination *and* definition are medical issues	51.3 (20)	0.0 (0)
2. Determination is a medical issue, definition involves other considerations	43.6 (17)	60 (9)
3. Definition is a medico-legal issue	33.3 (13)	26.7 (4)
4. Definition is a bio-ethical issue	25.6 (10)	40 (6)
5. Definition is a social or public issue	15.4 (6)	66.7 (10)
6. Definition is a philosophical and ethical issue	7.7 (3)	66.7 (10)

definition moves to a level which is more medico-technical, but not wholly so. Philosophical issues persist in the choice to define death in terms of organ systems, physiological functions, or recognizable human activities, capacities and conditions. (Capron and Kass, 1972, p. 102)

Finally, one would have to accept that individual medical professionals should be vested with the authority to change public policy on an area as fundamental as life and death. This no one would be willing to tolerate. (Veatch, 1972, p. 13)

Advances in medicine have accelerated development of techniques that will allow the physician to define and diagnose cerebral death with accuracy and rapidity in an appropriate hospital setting. (Korien, 1973, p. 14)

Utalitarian concerns, as well as an urgent preparedness to act characterized most of the medical articles; physicians wanted to get on with the definition in order to release organs as well as other scarce resources to the community at large. It would be a mistake, however, to imply that physicians did not raise any other ethical matters; they were particularly concerned with explicit codes of medical ethics and the ethics involved in transplantation procedures.

On the other hand, many of the ethicists trained in theology assumed a strikingly nonutilitarian posture, a posture not inconsistent with an ethics grounded in theology rather than the philosophy of social action. Several different levels of meaning comprise the concept of death, they argued, some of which are irreducibly philosophical and ethical in kind. Caution, open public debate, and conceptual and ethical clarity were the ingredients of their advocacy.

In the general terms of relative percentages, these differences hold, however oversimple they may be. But a word on the simplicity of these terms, as many as 20% of the physicians in the sample took a conservative, conceptually and ethically interpretive approach.

What of the senile who populate our rest homes and mental institutions? Such patients are also a drain on family and society. They, too, have a hopeless prognosis and have suffered deaths of portions of their brains. Change the legal definition of death a bit more and they, too, will be dead! (Toole, 1967, p. 603)

Likewise, a few of the ethicists were rather more radical and utilitarian than the rest.

Squirm as we may to avoid the inevitable, it seems time to admit to ourselves that there is simply no hiding place and that we must shoulder the responsibility of deciding to act in such a way as to hasten the declining trajectories of some lives, while doing our best to slow down the decline of others. (Morison, 1971)

CONCEPTUALIZATION AND IDEOLOGY

Can we consider the differences discussed above simply to be matters of conceptual difference, just two different modes of interpretation with little relation to ideology? One further example should suggest that even simple conceptual distinctions support ideological positions whether explicitly intended or not.

A relatively minor issue in the debate between ethicists and physicians was whether death could be considered a process or an event. This query, at first glance purely academic, reveals profound disagreements over the redefinition of death (see Morison, 1971; Kass, 1971). Those who assume that death is a process assume that different parts of the body die at different times. At which point then is death irreversible? If death is a relative matter, then some people are "more dead" than others, and one can then weigh the comparative worth of human lives. This conceptual stance focuses on the death of cells or organs, rather than on the death of persons. If defining death means deciding which cells and organs are dead, then those determinations are medical ones; redefining death becomes a medical issue, guts, feathers, and all. And, as a matter of fact, more physicians than ethicists drew the issue in these terms.

The other position, that death means the cessation of the functioning of the whole organism, directs one's concern to the dying individual.

> The body is as uniquely the body of this brain and no other, as the brain is as uniquely the brain of this body and no other. . . . My identity is the identity of the whole organism, even if the higher functions of personhood are seated in the brain. How else would a man love a woman and not merely her brains? How else could we lose ourselves in the aspect of a face? Be touched by the delicacy of a frame? . . . the body of the comatose, so long as—even with the help of art—it still breathes, pulses, and functions otherwise must still be considered a residual continuance of the subject that loved and was loved, and as such is still unentitled to some of the sacrosanctity accorded to such a subject by the laws of God and men. That sacrosanctity decrees that it must not be used as a mere means. (Jonas, 1974, p. 139)

And ethicists, who most often took this position, were less willing to participate in debates on the relative worth of lives and the common good.

MOTIVES AND INTERESTS: TECHNOLOGICAL IMPERATIVE VS. REFLECTIVE CRITIQUE

Physicians clearly wanted to resolve the matter to further the advance of medical practice. And ethicists sounded at times as if they alone were the few remaining champions of traditional human values. Moreover, if physicians assumed an attitude of urgent, imperative pragmatism, ethicists assumed one of reflective critique. Ethicists discussed some medical issues, such as the physiological criteria for determining death, but most often in conducting a critique of physicians' muddied reasoning or problematic ethics. They acted as conceptual and ethical critics as often, if not more often than they acted as advocates. I will give just a few examples of their conceptual (a-d) and ethical (e) critiques: (a) The concept of death differs from the criteria utilized to determine death. Updating the criteria does not necessarily justify updating the concept. (b) Identifying the death of a person with the death of his or her brain is reductionistic. (c) The question, When is death? is conceptually distinct from the question, When should a person be allowed to die? (For the first several years of the redefining process, and even today, the questions are not adequately distinguished.) (d) Scientific or technological assumptions and methods are inappropriate tools for the resolution of an essentially moral and philosophical issue ("The responsibility of a value-laden decision is replaced by the mechanics of a value-free routine" [Jonas, 1974]). (e) The definition of death should not be designed or enforced with reference to pragmatic or utilitarian matters such as costs, transplantation or the allocation of scarce resources.

> If no person's death should *for this purpose* be hastened, then the definition of death should *for this purpose* be updated, or the procedures for stating that a man has died be revised as a means of affording easier access to organs. (Ramsey, 1970, p. 103)

Both groups, as good professionals usually do, display both altruism and self-serving interest. Physicians' altruism lay in helping those in need of organs. If utilitarianism can be considered a form of altruism, then their altruism extended to their regard for the community at large.

There is more to transplantation than altruism, however—medical prestige, reward, and power come to transplant surgeons and hospitals with transplant programs. The early years of the defining process, 1966-1970, were also the years of the heart transplant, and who can forget the extraordinary honor and acclaim awarded heart transplant surgeons and teams?

In addition, we should not overlook the enormous cultural authority and control granted the medical profession over health, life, and death. One needn't strain to understand why they would consider the redefinition of death as existing wholly within their cultural ground of expertise: it serves their professional autonomy and control over such matters to do so. Dorothy Smith (1974) interprets ideology to mean "the interested procedures which people use as a means not to know" (quoted in Tuchman, 1978, p. 179). Missing a distinction between concept and criteria, or between the death of a person and the death of a brain, defining death as a process rather than an event, and interpreting the issue in terms of technological and medical solutions, are all conceptualizations which keep the issue bound in their cultural jurisdiction.

The ethicists' altruism was expressed in their insistence that the dying and their bodies be protected against the social benefits which derive from their deaths. And insofar as they supported public discussion of the meaning of death, their position was egalitarian. Their claims to the management of the redefining process can be considered to serve their interests in becoming more visible and influential in public discussions of contemporary moral dilemmas in health and technology.

Typical of the sort of professional ideology Schudson has described (1980), physicians' arguments were oriented to a beneficent control of the redefining process. Ethicists, too, had their points to make. However, the ethicist critique was liberating critique. They cleared the conceptual morass and maintained a clear vision of the basic meanings of the human situation, of being and having a body.

Habermas (1971) distinguishes three types of knowledge interests: technical, pragmatic, and emancipatory. Knowledge, according to Habermas, in the critical or emancipatory mode is the only knowledge which can be freed from human interests. On these bases, I would suggest that it is technical interests which forms the physicians' position. It is practical and emancipatory interest which informs the ethicists' advocacy and criticism.

DIALOGUE OR DOMINATION?

Though thus far, the relation between physicians and ethicists has been drawn as one of professional debate, exchange and discourse between them occurred most frequently in committee and symposia meetings. Otherwise, domination through neglect and omission generally characterized the relationship. When asked about their discussion of death with others, physicians said they wrote for physicians, that they read only the medical journals, and that other physicians had been influential in their thinking on the matter. Ethicists, on the other hand, said they intended their work to address members of each of the professions, as well as policy-makers and the lay public. They said they read important legal and medical journals, as well as ethical and philosophical journals, and that physicians had been influential in their thinking. The communication pattern that emerges resembles a hierarchy of exclusion, with physicians at the top addressing, and listening to their own colleagues, and ethicists at the bottom addressing and receiving a variety of groups and interests.

The ethicist critique has only recently caught on among physicians, and then among relatively few, even though the criticism has appeared in publications widely read by physicians. How can we make sense of the neglect or omission of the ethicist critique? First, in keeping with some of their other assumptions, perhaps physicians did not consider the ethical challenge to be either important or to the point. And second, perhaps some conceptual distinctions and ethical arguments are simply too fragile and impalpable against the prevailing pragmatic and technological ethos governing the definition of contemporary moral dilemmas.

Clearly, ideology characterizes professional, scientific debate—in expressions of professional altruism and professional interests toward both control and critique of the definition. And in this case, I would say, after Habermas, that ideology extends deeply into the ground of unexamined conceptualization.

REFERENCES

CAPRON, A. and L. KASS (1972). A Statutory Definition of the Standards for Determining Human Death: An Appraisal and a Proposal, *University of Pennsylvania L.R.*, 121.

CORBETT, L. (1974). The Diagnosis of Cerebral Death in the Community Hospital, *Journal of AOA*, 74.

GOULDNER, A. (1976). "The Dialectric of Ideology and Technology." New York: Seabury Press.

HABERMAS, J. (1970). Technology and science as "Ideology." *In* J. Habermas, "Toward a Rational Society." Boston, MA: Beacon Press.

HABERMAS, J. (1971). "Knowledge and Human Interests.," Boston, MA: Beacon Press.

JOHNSON, T. (1977). "Professions and Power." London: MacMillan.

JONAS, H. (1974). Against the Stream: Comments on the Definition and Redefinition of Death, "Philosophical Essays" (Englewood Cliffs, NJ: Prentice-Hall).

KASS, L. (1971). Death as an Event: A Commentary on Robert Morison, *Science*, 173.

KOREIN, J. (1973). On Cerebral, Brain and Systematic Death, *Current Concepts of Cerebrovascular Disease and Stroke*, 8 (3).

LOWREY, J. (1971). Changing Concepts of Death, *Hawaii Medical Journal*, 30 (4).

LUCHI, R. (1971). Diagnosis of Cerebral Death, *Journal of the Iowa Medical Society*, 61.

MARCUSE, H. (1968). "Negations." Boston, MA: Beacon Press.

MORISON, R. (1971). Death: Process or Event, *Science*, 170.

PAULSON, G. (1972). Determination of Brain Death, *Ohio State Medical Journal*.

RADO, L. (1979). "Communication, Social Organization and Redefinition of Death." Unpublished dessertation, University of Pennsylvania.

RADO, L. (1981). Death redefined: Social and cultural influences on legislation. *Journal of Communication 31* (No. 1), 41-47.

RAMSEY, P. (1970). On Updating Procedures for Stating That A Man Has Died, "The Patient as Person" New Haven, CT: Yale University Press.

SCHUDSON, M. (1978). "Discovering the News." New York: Basic Books.

SCHUDSON, M. (1980). A discussion of Magali Sarfatti Larson's *The Rise of Professionalism: A Sociological Analysis. Theory and Society 9*, 215-229.

SMITH, D. (1974). Theorizing as ideology." *In* R. Turner (Ed.), "Ethnomethodology." Middlesex, England: Penguin.

TOOLE, J. (1967). Danger Ahead: Problems in Defining Life and Death, *North Carolina Medical Journal*.

TUCHMAN, G. (1978). "Making News." New York: Free Press.

VEATCH, R. (1972). Brain Death—Welcome Definition or Dangerous Judgment? *Hastings Center Report*, November.

12

The Problem of Ideology:
Some Necessary Distinctions

NICHOLAS GARNHAM
Polytechnic of Central London
London WIP 7PD England

As Perry Anderson (1976) has pointed out in his *Considerations on Western Marxism*, there has been a marked tendency within Western Marxism to focus upon the study of the superstructure, upon culture, upon ideology. The reasons for that emphasis, its roots in the Left's political failures in the 1920s and 1930s, and in capitalism's long post-war boom have been well enough analyzed.

My purpose in this paper is not to criticize that development as such, which, for all its one-sidedness, has brought undoubted political and intellectual gains. In my estimation, it is an intellectual tide that has already turned. What will be examined are some of the problems raised by the study of ideology, or, rather, by the study of social formations from the perspective of ideology, and the ways in which those problems are often glossed over because of the very terms used to conduct the analysis. The word ideology, I suggest, has in recent years been widely used in left-oriented study of the media in an extremely loose, imprecise, and, thus, analytically obfuscatory way; a situation made worse by the currently fashionable substitution of the term "discourse" for "ideology."

We are faced here immediately with one of the central problems for cultural analysis, the polysemic nature of language and the fact that both the object of our analysis (in so far as it is embodied in language and, to a very large extent, it is), and also our tools of analysis are themselves at stake, both in the process of social struggle and in the process of its resulting historical change.

One is forced to use words like "ideology and culture," knowing well, and in spite of, their imprecision of meaning, because there are no others with which to pin down the relevant processes. Thus, one is caught in the bind of using a vocabulary while simultaneously criticizing it.

First, an important analytical distinction must be drawn between what Jorge Larrain has called the positive and negative notions of ideology.

Marx's own usage of ideology was the negative one. That is to say, he used the term ideology in a precise and restricted sense to mean a structured set of ideas about the world which were both objectively false (that is to say their falsity could be demonstrated by science) and in the interest of the dominant class. His example was vulgar political economy.

This immediately raises a number of important distinctions.

1. Between true ideas and false ideas and how such a distinction can be grounded.
2. Between ideas that are in the interest of the dominant class and those that are not, which is a matter of empirical historical analysis and political judgement.

It is worth noting, particularly in view of the strong anti-science current on the Left, that Marx himself was a rationalist, and I suspect that for him true ideas could never, in the long term, be in the interest of the dominant class.

The real problems begin with the positive view of ideology, since it is this view, in a strange mixture with the restricted, negative view, which informs most current Leftist usage of the term.

This view, which can be found in Lenin, Lukacs, Gramsci, and Goldman, derives in part from non-Marxist, idealist sources such as Dilthey, Weber, and Durkheim. In this view, ideology is a structured world view shared by a distinct social group. The question of truth and falsity is open, and, in some versions, so are the directions of social determinacy, i.e., did Protestantism cause the rise of the capitalist bourgeoisie or vice-versa? In this view the world is one of *contending* ideologies, the function of ideology being to provide normative social cohesion by providing an acceptable and accepted explanation of the world.

This tradition, true to its idealist roots, tends to over-value both the power of ideas and their coherence; hence, no doubt, its attraction for intellectuals.

A second, related problem involves the notions of social being and social consciousness and their relation of determination. Although they are distinct, the distinction is widely suppressed in that school of Marxist analysis associated with Althusser, among others, which wishes to locate ideology in practice.

The question here is not whether or not we can distinguish consciousness from the symbolic realm. For the present purpose, I will assume that consciousness has its being at the level of the symbolic. Now, the crucial point to be made about symbols, the source of their immense productive power, is that they are non-material and have no necessary relationship to the material world. To this extent the idealist tradition is correct. This power, as has often been pointed out, is epitomized by the function of negation, the ability to say NO.

A crude example illustrates the implications of this for debates about ideology. Daily work on a production line has historically produced (at the level of consciousness) the whole range from an active socialist militant to a company "fink." The practice itself does not determine in that sense the meaning that any individual makes of that practice.

This is not, of course, to deny that our world, in this case the production line and capitalist relations of production, is not materialized consciousness—that is to say a distinct set of ideas given concrete form—nor that a given form of material practice sets very real limits to the probability of given forms of historical consciousness arising. The point is that there is a necessary relative autonomy between being and consciousness, such that the latter cannot simply be read off from the former but always requires concrete, empirical historical analysis.

But the problem of the consciousness/being or ideology/practice relationship raises other questions, showing the need for other distinctions; in particular, that between individual consciousness and social consciousness. For it is not merely that the practice of production line work and the consciousness materialized in that practice determines a given individual's consciousness. So does the given historical state of the symbolic realm itself. To this extent the notion of ideological practice points to something important. We think, we come to consciousness with the symbolic tools at our disposal. This raises the problem of the differing and historically determinant modes by which the symbolic realm is itself determined. At one level there are material, biological determinants, the receptivity of the human senses, the effects of malnutrition on mental development, etc.; at another level, there are the determinants of the structure of language and of other codified or semi-codified symbolic forms. These, I would suggest, develop over time spans and to rhythms quite other than, although effected by, those of the even long-term epochal changes such as feudalism and capitalism. Thus while the input of linguistics into the study of ideological phenomena has undoubtedly been fruitful, the exaggeration of the linguistic model has not. To talk of language as an ideology, or even as the key basis of ideology, seems to me both scientifically and politically harmful. Clearly, linguistic styles, often at an unconscious level, contain distinct views of the world. Nonetheless, even in those cases the degree of determinacy over what is expressed and understood by others should not be exaggerated.

But this leads to another level of determinacy in the symbolic realm. It seems that the distinction within Marx's notion of ideology between (a), ideas as such, and (b), structured sets of ideas with a certain level of social currency, is a distinction we need to maintain. With such a distinction we can analyze both the social forces that structure ideas and give them social currency on the one hand, and on the other hand, the relationship between those structured, socially available sets of ideas and the ideas which individual social actors hold.

We cannot assume the relation of determinacy between the structuring and social dissemination process, roughly the work of intellectuals and cultural institutions, and the everyday ideas of individuals and social groups. Moreover, different modes of analysis may be necessary to explain why certain ideas are structured in certain ways and how and why they are distributed.

This last point urges consideration of the mass-media. While the symbolic is distinct from the material, if ideas are to acquire social currency, they require a material carrier. But again the analysis of the material practice involved in this process of dissemination, a process that includes the moment of what is sometimes called creation and that of consumption or reading, must be distinguished from analysis of the social effectivity of the ideas as such. We cannot assume that a system of dissemination determined at the economic material level by the capitalist mode of production will necessarily carry a set of ideas tending to reproduce that mode. Indeed, in my view, the economic and ideological needs of the dominant class may be, often in fact are, in conflict.

In summary, we need to make a range of distinctions within the field covered by the term ideology:

1. Between being and consciousness, between practice and ideas;
2. Between individual consciousness and structured, coherent, socially available sets of ideas;
3. Between sets of ideas that are true and those that are false;
4. Between those ideas the dissemination of which favor the dominant class and those which do not;
5. Between the normative values of a social group and its consciously held ideas about the world;
6. Between the symbolic realm and its processes, on the one hand, and the material practices by means of which the symbolic is embodied and circulated, on the other.

We need to remember that what people think and what they do may be different matters.

REFERENCE

ANDERSON, P. (1976). "Considerations on Western Marxism." London: NLB.

13

Communication, Fetishism, and Ideology

GORDON WELTY
Wright State University
Dayton, Ohio 45431

Frederick Engels, in his 1883 "Speech at the Graveside of Karl Marx," compared Marx's discovery of the law of development of human history to Darwin's discovery of the law of development of organic nature. The terms of this comparison suggest two points about the law of development of history: first, that Marx's understanding of this law was not confined to bourgeois society; and second, that our understanding of this law may be enlarged by considering Darwin's taxonomic approach to biology. As Karl Linné had systematized biological organisms into the Linnaean taxonomy, so the predecessors of historical materialism had systematized social forms (e.g., Montesquieu—see Huxley, 1964, p. 390ff)—but only superficially. Not until the research of Marx, Engels, and Morgan was the law of development of the history (the phylogeny and logic) of social forms (the social *taxa*) established in a thoroughgoing materialist and historical fashion.

Now the law of development of human history holds that social forms move in their social antagonisms. Thus the most basic category of a Marxian taxonomy, the level of an *order*, is the category of social antagonism. The antagonistic social order is preceded and followed by nonantagonistic social orders. At this basic level, Marx's law is an instance of the dialectic of the Immediate, the Mediate, and the Mediated Immediate (Gould, 1980, p. 3ff). These are the moments of the unrelated unity of Sein-an-sich, the nonantagonistic community; the externally related disunity of Sein-für-anderes, the various antagonistic social forms; and finally the reconstituted unity of Sein-an und für-sich, the ethical community of direct producers. These three social orders, constituting the most fundamental level of differentiation of society, can be schematized as follows.

The law of development of human history further holds that social

FIGURE 1

PRE-ANTAGONISTIC	ANTAGONISTIC	NON-ANTAGONISTIC
DIALECTICAL MOMENTS SEIN-AN-SICH	SEIN-FÜR-ANDERES	SEIN-AN-UND FÜR-SICH

FIGURE 2

	I	II	III
FORMS OF APPROPRIATION	Taxes	Rent	Profit
FORMS OF PROPERTY	Communal	Private	Capitalist
FORMS OF SERVITUDE	General Slavery	Serfdom and Chattel Slavery	Wage-Labor

FORMS OF APPEARANCE OF SOCIAL ANTAGONISM

antagonism appears in several forms. Thus, the next level, *genus*, is subsumed within the orders of society. Marx's February 1881 drafts of his letter to Zasulich suggested that there have been successively three *genera* (or fundamental formations) of the antagonistic order of society, and he defined these as the *forms of property:* communal property in land, then individualized private property, and finally capitalistic private property. Soon thereafter, in the *Origin of the Family,* Engels (1972, p. 234) provided a corresponding discussion of "the three great epochs of civilization," where the epochs were defined in terms of the *social division of labor:* slavery, then serfdom, and finally wage labor. Finally, in *Capital,* Marx (1962, Vol. 3, pp. 798-799) differentiated three forms of appropriation of surplus labor: taxes, rent *per se,* and profits. Of course, all these forms of appearance of social antagonism are correlated. The three *genera* of antagonistic society and the forms of appearance of their antagonism can be schematized as follows.

Finally, the law of development of human history holds that the forms of appearance of social antagonisms are actualized under specific ecological, climatic, and other conditions in specific socioeconomic formations. Thus, the final category of a Marxian taxonomy, the level of *species*, is subsumed within the *genera* of society. These species make up the familiar series of gentile, Asiatic, ancient, feudal, and bourgeois formations. The evolution of the specific pre-antagonistic social forms was discussed in Morgan's *Ancient Society*, Marx's *Ethnological Notebooks*, and Engels' *Origin of the Family*. The evolution of the specific socioeconomic formations within the *genus* of communal property and general slave forms, from the patriarchal tribal species up to the Asiatic species, was briefly discussed in Marx's draft letters to Zasulich and in Engel's *Anti-Dühring*. Likewise, specific formations evolved within the *genus* of individual private property, from the ancient Greek and Roman species through the medieval feudal species up to the early mercantile species. Finally, the evolution of the specific formations within the *genus* of capitalistic property, from the competitive capitalistic species up to the imperialist species, was discussed in Volume 1 of Marx's *Capital*, and in Lenin's *Development of Capitalism in Russia* and his *Imperialism*. All these species of social forms and their *genera* can be schematized as follows.

The theoretical task of historical materialism is two-fold: first, dialectially to derive, in terms of an historical materialist categorematics, from the orders of antagonistic and non-antagonistic societies the *genera* or fundamental formations, and to derive the socioeconomic varieties from the *species;* and second, to discover the essential unity of the varieties within the range of appearances of the historical instances. For the present purposes, the schematized taxonomy will suffice to analyse the origins of fetishisms and ideologies, and perhaps to dispel the oft-repeated charges against Marxism of "mechanistic theory," "eclecticism," etc. (See, e.g., Amin, 1972, p. 234; for a further discussion of the Marxian taxonomy, see Welty, forthcoming.)

A form of social antagonism necessarily has its own *reflection* in the ideational sphere and hence in the consciouness of the participants in the antagonistic relationships. This ideational reflection on the one side is *general*, whereby the relationship of subject to object is inverted; this general reflection of antagonism is *ideology*. On the other side, the reflection is *particular*, whereby the part is taken for the whole; this particular reflection of antagonism is the *fetish*. The systematization of the fetish is the *fetishism*, which constitutes the *specificity* of the distortion of the ideational sphere.

Ideologies are customarily dichotomized into the *sacred* and the *secular*, the *traditional* and the *modern*. The general aspect of the former is, of course, *religious* or *sacred ideology*, and the particular aspect is the *religious fetish*. Within the first *genus* of antagonistic society where this ideology first emerges, the conjunction of the communal form of property and social antagonisms necessitates a further specification of control over labor power and its product. Hence the specific aspect of this ideology is *patriarchalism* or *Amazonism* (Kanter, 1926, p. 72ff). Thereby the control of the fetishes, and

FIGURE 3   Genera and Species of Society

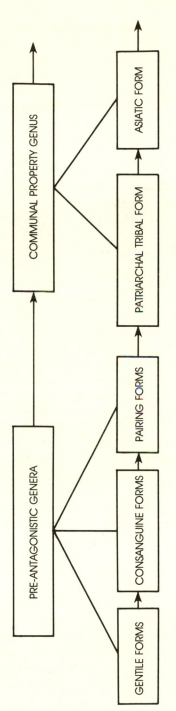
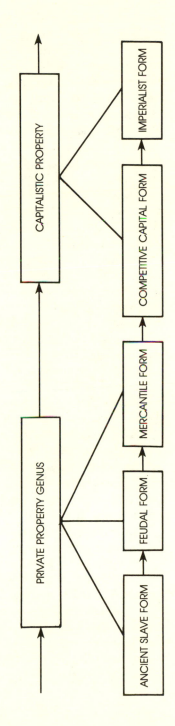

not incidentally, labor power and labor product, is justified in terms iso-
morphic to those of the ideology in general.

The more astute of the bourgeois writers, e.g., Eliade (1959, pp. 23-
24), find the necessity of acknowledging a third, intermediate ideology which
is neither sacred nor secular. Interestingly enough, Marx had already identified the specific fetishism which corresponds to this ideology in his *1844
Manuscripts: land fetishism* which was characteristic of mercantilism and
physiocracy. The general aspect of this ideology of individual private property
is the *philosophy* of natural law which dominated Western thought from the
time of Aristotle, through Aquinas, up to the time of the American War of
Independence. The particular or fetish aspect is the *land*, the private property
of the citizen, the demesne of the feudal lord, the *patria* which evolves into
the national state. Within the second *genus* of antagonistic society, patriarchalism still served to justify control of labor power within the household or
estate, but the newly emerged social relations (e.g., individual exchange)
necessitated a new specificity of ideology. This specific aspect was "political
science" justifying the control of "la grande famille" while subsuming the
patriarchal control of "la petite famille." Likewise natural law rationalized
religious ideology, generating Christianity. These subsumptions illustrate
the tendency of the ideology of one *genus* to transcend and sublate the
ideology of a prior *genus*, just as do the real conditions of that *genus*.

Finally, the particular aspcet of modern ideology is the *commodity fetish;*
its systematization is specifically *bourgeois economics*. Since the time of
Comte, bourgeois ideology has recognized the limitations of bourgeois economics and has sought a more general "science of society" or sociology, the
general aspect of modern ideology (Comte, 1839, Vol. 4, p. 264ff). The false
totalization of general sociology has been attempted by Weber (1978, p. 63ff)
(resp. Menger's economics), by Pareto (1963, p. 1142ff) (resp. his own economics), and by Parsons (1932, 1949) (resp. Marshall's economics), to mention
only a few examples.

Within the third *genus*, patriarchalism and patriotism provide important
labor force justifications for control, but the complex exigencies of the de-
veloping class struggle call for the complete rationalization of these doctrines.
Likewise, the general aspect of third *genus* ideology subsume its predecessors
through the Sociology of Religion, and the Sociology of Knowledge.

All these aspects of ideology, from sacred to secular, and the *genera* of
antagonistic society they reflect, can be schematized as follows.

This recapitulates the prehistory (or phylogeny) of the forms of ideology
and fetishism, providing an historical materialist sketch of the origins as well
as the interrelationships of these forms (Welty, forthcoming, chapter 3).
Subsequent to the prehistory of a social form is its history, the examination
of the logic of the reproduction process of the explicit or fully developed
form.

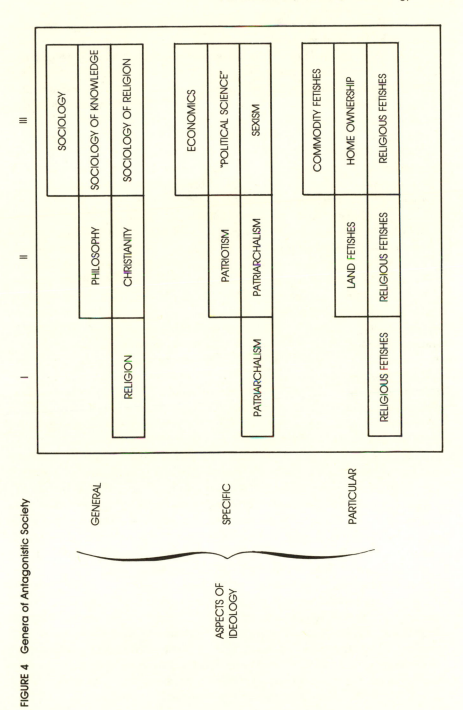

FIGURE 4 Genera of Antagonistic Society

The communication process of cultural transmission has four essential aspects, the cultural *agent* (the accultured), the cultural *patient* (or acculturee), the cultural *medium* (or artifact), and the cultural *message* (or meaning). Taken together, these aspects constitute a mode of communication. The essence of the last of the aspects of this mode of communication, the meaning of ideology and fetishism, has already been noted as the inversion of the relationship of subject and object and the confusion of part and whole, to justify privatized control of labor power and labor product. Further, the transmission of ideology and fetishism in all three *genera* of antagonistic society has implicated essentially the same cultural agents and patients, viz. the older and the younger generation. Hence the essential differences of the ideological communication process at the level of the social *genus* must be discovered in the differential media.

In his *Empire and Communication,* Innis (1972) has made a suggestive study of the effect of variation in the media of communication on the rest of the culture sphere. He held that the medium of communication influenced cultural transmission over space and time, and the relative spatial or temporal emphasis implies a significant *bias* both to the cultural transmission and to the culture itself. A heavy, durable, and relatively immobile medium is better suited to cultural transmission through time, while a light, easily transported medium is better suited to cultural transmission through space. Monumental architecture, for instance, is the transmission of culture in the medium of stone and promotes a temporal bias, an assertion of hegemony through sheer permanence. Hence the characteristic cultural tendencies of first *genus* societies, such as ancient Egypt and Babylon. Temporal bias reinforces religious fetishism through the emergence of temple architecture and a priestly caste; this fetishism is to a lesser extent enhanced by the spatial bias deriving from despotic centralization. Papyrus rolls, by contrast, facilitate cultural transmission in the written media and tend more toward a spatial bias, an assertion of hegemony across large and heterogeneous areas through imperial administration. Hence the characteristic cultural tendencies of second *genus* societies, which nonetheless retained some of the sense of permanence. Radio, the cinema, and television promote the transmission of culture in the mass or postliterate media and are intensely spatially biased; hence the charcteristic cultural and ideological tendencies of third *genus* societies, which still retain some of the same of permanence and heterogeneity. This intense spatial bias reinforces commodity fetishism by promoting synchronic human interactions, thereby rendering interactions equivalent; the far less salient temporal bias also enhances commodity fetishism through the increasing capitalization of the communications industry, whereby the rising organic composition of that capital provides a strong technological impetus to the development of the media and the several genres as cultural *forms* which far outstrip their cultural *content.*

The resulting distribution of ideology is far from homogeneous. It can be characterized in terms of the primary antagonistic social relations of bourgeois society, sex, and class. Religious fetishism is more prevalent among women than men.[1] Land fetishism is more prevalent among the subordinate classes than in the bourgeoisie.[2] In some part, these specific differences within the modern ideological unity of religious, land, and commodity fetishism reflect differences of formal and informal education. In a more important part, these differences reflect different interests. For instance, the heightened commodity fetishism of the bourgeois means he is less encumbered by patriotism; this is compatible with the exigencies of multinational enterprise, "runaway" corporations, the employment of "Guestarbeiten," and imperialist adventure.[3] The heightened land fetishism of the working class (and other subordinate classes) means they can justify their privatized attempts to avoid total subjugation to capital, leading to "home ownership," national chauvinism, etc.[4] The heightened religious fetishism of woman means she can justify her self-alienation in family planning and in childbirth; this is compatible with the woman's avoidance of total subjugation to capital, through childrearing and the widely documented primacy she gives to household demands over the workplace (Komarovsky, 1967; Lopata, 1971). Retrograde though these strivings may be, they are the ideological reflections of the exigence that "the proletariat cannot liberate itself as a class without simultaneously abolishing class society" (Lukács, 1971, p. 70).

It must be acknowledged that this discussion of ideology and fetishism has been cast at the level of the social *genus*, rather than that of specific social formations and their varieties. This level of discussion has been necessitated by the present situation.[5] Even at this level it is possible to clarify the relationship between ideological forms such as sexism, religion, commodity fetishism, etc.

---

[1] The author participated in the 1975 global poll described in Gallup (1976-1977). Random samples of respondents from Western Europe and North America answered questions about religious affiliation, importance of personal religious beliefs, and beliefs in immorality, and in the existence of God. A greater percentage of women than men in each of these nations evidenced religiosity on each of these items.

[2] Perhaps needless to stress, public opinion polls are unable to provide direct evidence for this proposition, due to the miniscule portion of the bourgeoisie in the general population if for no other reason. It is suggestive, however, that the masses' lack of information on foreign policy issues gives them a parochial orientation while rendering them vulnerable to jingoist manipulation by the bourgeois and their ideologists. The limited perspective of the masses is conducive to land fetishism while the manipulative activity of the bourgeoisie is not.

[3] Alexis de Tocqueville (1969, p. 258) observed, "I have come across real patriotism among the people but have often looked in vain for any such thing among their rulers."

[4] See Engels (1935); for a discussion of land fetishism as it relates to another of the subordinate groups, viz. family farmers, see Mann and Dickinson (1978).

[5] Further discussion of these topics is contained in Welty (1982).

REFERENCES

AMIN, S. (1974). "Accumulation on a World Scale." New York: Monthly Review Press.

COMTE, A. (1839). "Cours de Philosophie Positive." Paris: Bachelier.

ELIADE, M. (1959). "The Sacred and the Profane." New York: Harcourt, Brace, Jovanovich.

ENGELS, F. (1935). "The Housing Question." New York: International Publishers.

ENGELS, F. (1972). "Origin of the Family, Private Property and the State." New York: International Publishers.

GALLUP, G. (1976-1977). Human needs and satisfactions: A global survey. *Public Opinion Quarterly 40*, 459-467.

GOULD, C. (1980). "Marx's Social Ontology." Cambridge, MA: MIT Press.

HUXLEY, J. (1964). "Evolution: The Modern Synthesis." New York: John Wiley.

INNIS, H.A. (1972). "Empire and Communication." Toronto, Ontario: University of Toronto Press.

KANTER, E. (1926). "The Amazons: A Marxian Study." Chicago, IL: Kerr.

KOMAROVSKY, M. (1967). "Blue-Collar Marriage." New York: Vintage Books.

LOPATA, H. (1971). "Occupation: Housewife." New York: Oxford University Press.

LUKÁCS, G. (1971). "History and Class Consciousness. Cambridge, MA: MIT Press.

MANN, S., and DICKINSON, J. (1978). Obstacles to the development of a capitalist agriculture. *Journal of Peasant Studies 5*, 466-481.

MARX, K. (1962). "Capital." Moscow, USSR: Foreign Languages Publishing House.

PARETO, V. (1963). "Mind and Society." New York: Dover.

PARSONS, T. (1932). Wants and activities in Marshall. *Quarterly Journal of Economics 46*, 101-140.

PARSONS, T. (1949). "The Structure of Social Action." New York: Free Press.

TOCQUEVILLE, A. de. (1969). "Democracy in America." Garden City, New York: Doubleday.

WEBER, M. (1978). "Economy and Society." Berkeley, CA: University of California Press.

WELTY, G. (1981). The materialist science of culture and the critique of ideology. *Quarterly Journal of Ideology 5*, 1-19.

WELTY, G. (Forthcoming). "Theory of Ideology." Amsterdam, Holland: B.F. Grüner.

14

Psycho-Social Dynamics and the Prospects for Mankind*

CHARLES E. OSGOOD
University of Illinois
Champaign, Illinois 61820

The Russell-Einstein Manifesto issued in 1955 on the 10th anniversary of the first nuclear bombing on Hiroshima, sets the theme for this contribution to what must surely be th greatest debate in human history.

> We are speaking on this occasion, not as member of this or that nation, continent or creed, but as human beings, members of the species Man, whose continued existence is in doubt. . . . We have to learn to think in a new way . . . to ask ourselves . . . what steps can be taken to prevent a military contest of which the issue must be disastrous to all parties . . . what perhaps impedes understanding of the situation more than anything else is that the term "mankind" feels vague and abstract. . . . We appeal, as human beings, to human beings: Remember your humanity, and forget the rest.

But have we learned in the last 25 years "to think in a new way"? The answer must be a resounding *"NO"!* And our "old ways of thinking" are having *causal,* not merely casual, relations to our failures to solve global problems. New ways of thinking don't "just happen;" they have to be acquired—and what I propose for this highly interdependent world is *mutual learning processes for some "new ways of thinking."*

I refer to certain dynamic processes in human thinking as the "Neanderthal Mentality" precisely because they are so primitive. Most of us recognize these processes in others but remain blissfully unaware of them in

---

*This paper is an up-dating of the essences of my presidential address to the Peace Science Society (International) in 1977 and an address (bearing the same title) at a UN Colloquium on The Societal Context of Disarmament in 1978.

ourselves. Escape from the constraints of these processes may come by recognizing their operation on our own thinking as well as on that of others.

Neanderthal Thinking

Perhaps the most primitive dynamic is what I call *Pollyannaism*—after the blindly optimistic heroine of a novel by Eleanor Porter early in this century. It is simply easier for humans to process affectively *positive* (pleasant, gratifying) things words, etc., than affectively *negative* (unpleasant, threatening) ones. I am reminded of a Frank and Ernest comic strip, in which Frank says: "Yesterday, for just one moment, all the world news came into focus for me and I got a glimpse of what is really happening. Boy! I hope that never happens again!"

In our own psycholinguistic research at the University of Illinois, we have shown that college subjects "simply get the meaning" of the positive members of word-pairs significantly quicker than of negative members (never shown *as* pairs, of course)—e.g., *joy* quicker than *pain*, *reward* quicker than *punish*, and *above* quicker than *below*. This finding has already been replicated with native Chinese speakers and is now being tested in three other languages—so it is beginning to appear that humans *are*, universally, Pollyannas!

Psycho-logic is a related dynamic—the easier mental processing of congruent as compared with incongruent sentences. When we experimentally compared congruent sentences, which must be conjoined by inserting "and" (e.g., *Tom is tall* ("and") *strong*), with incongruent ones, which must be conjoined by "but" (e.g., *Tom is tall* ("but") *weak*), we found that congruent "and"s were much more quickly produced than incongruent "buts"s. Utilizing research in 12 of the 30 diversified language-culture communities included in the 20-year project of our Center for Comparative Psycholinguistics, we find that *dynamics of primitive psycho-logic are* (apparently) *human universals.*

Psycho-logic phenomena are also very familiar (and critical) in the real world outside the laboratory, of course. For example, Psycho-logic runs rampant in international relations. Exactly the *same* behavior—like sending (potential) combat troops to friendly nations bordering on an enemy, as in Turkey—is acceptable if the noble WE's do it, but completely unacceptable if the bestial THEY's do it, as in Cuba. Thus the Neanderthal within strives to force a complicated world into an oversimplified mold, grossly distorting it in the process.

Cognitive Stereotypy is yet another psycho-logic dynamism. As our Neanderthal's emotional stress increases beyond some optimum level, his or her stronger (most habitual) tendencies become relatively more and the weaker (least habitual) relatively less so—a shift *toward* blind stereotypy and *away from* creative flexibility. Thus, paradoxically, the greater the anxiety and the *need* for a novel solution to a problem, the *less likely* the Neanderthal mentality is to discover it.

A recent study by Peter Suedfeld et al. (1977) seems peculiarly apropos here. Applying a type of content analysis (designed to index "integrative complexity") to UN speeches by representatives of both Israel and the United Arab Republics, they were able to show that cognitive complexity dipped sharply during periods of conflict, reaching low points in 1948, 1956, 1967, and 1973—precisely preceding outbreaks of conflict.

Two *Reinforcement* principles—familiar to psychologists working in both animal and human laboratories—concern the effectiveness of reinforcement, either positive (reward) or negative (punishment), in inducing changes in thinking and behaving: first, that *immediate reinforcement is more effective than remote;* second, that *concrete reinforcement is more effective than symbolic.* For the problems that face mankind today, these tend to be cor-related—the more *immediate* tending to be the more *concrete* (money in the hand for a profitable arms contract) and the more *remote* tending to be the more *symbolic* (nuclear war resulting from proliferation of nuclear power technology).

Now, when Pollyannaism combines with these Reinforcement factors, one gets a very frightening interaction: the more people can avoid thinking about Negatives (like a nuclear accident or there being no more fuel for cars)—particularly when they seem remote in time and are highly symbolic in nature—the *less* likely they are to try to do anything about them until it's too late. Seated in the backyard on a nice spring day, watching the kids at play, and sipping a beer, the Neanderthal within us simply cannot conceive of the trees suddenly blackened and the voices of the children stilled—or of there being no more beer.

Human Talking (and Writing)

Some very fundamental changes in the meanings humans—in high places as well as low—have for the crucial economic, social, and political symbols of our time will be required, if mankind is to reach the year 2000 in anything like its present shape.

I have pointed out elsewhere (Osgood, 1971) the gap between word and thing increases with the thing's *remoteness* from immediate experience; that the words of international politics are typically *analogic* (human "We's" and "They's," "trust" or "defy" each other, and there are "slippery slopes" and physical "rows of dominos"); that the power of words lies in the ways they *abstract from reality,* sharpening certain features and leveling others (thus "pencils" are to write with, not to kindle fires with, and one can freeze to death for lack of kindling wood with a pocketful of wooden pencils!); and that we are being led by old men using antiquated semantic maps to guide us through the wonderland of the 20th century.

The power of sentences lies in the fact that they can be used to assert things about their topics ("*Russians* can't be trusted"); that they can "crunch" words together and change their meanings ("He's a *Fifth-amendment* Communist"); and that they *are* potentially radical—lending themselves to concisely vivid expressions (like "*She* will make someone a nice husband")—thereby stimulating fresh ways of thinking.

There must be "rules for breaking rules" in sentencing (e.g., to produce apposite metaphors like "Billboards are *warts* on the face of the countryside" rather than mind-boggling ones like "the summer breeze *shouted* down the valley"). One must maintain a healthy suspicion of pat phrases (like "mutual nuclear deterrence" and "civil defense"). *The most important ingredient in a semantic revolution is using radical sentences to compensate for conservative words.* For example, consider the following illustration: "the usual motive behind the threatening behavior of one nation toward another is fear," "there is no real security in military superiority in a nuclear age," "mutual trust is a result of, rather than a prerequisite for, de-escalation of tensions," and "nations cannot retain unlimited national sovereignty while at the same time attaining international security."

SUBJECTIVE CAUSES OF MANKIND'S OBJECTIVE PROBLEMS

Science and Technology. Between the mid 1960s and the mid 1970s, the military-industrial complex experienced a subtle shift from *the goal of disarmament to the concept of arms control*—a concept which puts no real ceiling on the arms race and promises very profitable competition and proliferation.

Jerome Frank (1977, p. 23) showed how the combination of *Pollyannaism* and *Symbolic-Remoteness of Reinforcement* contribute to nuclear proliferation.

> National leaders, in general, are optimists—that is, they believe that the course of action which they have determined will succeed. . . . Moreover, the dangers of nuclear proliferation are not real psychologically because they are indefinite and distant in time. . . . A calculation of the positive and negative consequences of promoting or regulating the spread of nuclear capabilities according to these principles unfortunately yields an overwhelming balance in favor of promotion.

In the face of escalating military budgets, accompanying despair over inflation, cutbacks in most domestic programs, and a frightening national debt, how does the Complex maintain its public support? There is a remarkable coincidence between heavily advertised "scare campaigns" and the pre-voting debates in the House and Senate—an application of *Immediate and Concrete Reinforcment*, for the public (fear of the Russian Bogey) and for their Congressional representatives (fear of losing support in elections).

It seems that a **collective** insanity exists, one that is shared by whole societies. If **individuals** were to display similar symptoms society would brand them as **paranoid**. But when Neanderthal thinking permeates a whole society, it is the **deviants** who are likely to be called "insane." Interestingly, Americans apply this reasoning to the Communists when they put *their* dissidents into mental institutions—but not to their own society.

Resources and the Environment.   Quoting George Wald (1975, p. 23):

> It is estimated that if we were to stop all use of spray-cans now, we will already [in 1975] have lost about 10 pecent of the ozone (layer). . . . (The) workplaces are at least as big a killer [as the automobile]. We register about 22,000 deaths by industrial accident every year, and 2.2 million disabling injuries—but those statistics don't touch the slow killing: the black lung . . . the brown lung . . . the silicosis, asbestosis, and uranium poisoning, and the variety of cancers associated with these conditions . . . such statistics are hard to come by, because industry fights tooth and nail to keep them concealed.

The problems of energy and environmental destruction/pollution are intimately related, of course.

According to Luther Carter (1977), if the growth of the nuclear power industry matches the Nuclear Regulatory Commission's (NRC) expectations, there will be more than 125,000 tons of nuclear waste from 500 large reactors by the year 2000—and this doesn't even include some 75 million gallons of military waste currently stored in about 200 underground tanks. All of this nuclear waste must be kept isolated from the biosphere for what, in our human perspective, is essentially *forever*. When, at the Atomic Energy Commission's request and funding, the National Academy of Sciences set up a committee in 1957 to study nuclear waste, the AEC suppressed its highly critical findings and cut off support.

National and International Social Structures.   In the past, Americans have reduced their standard of living, at times of war and during the great depression, but now they must be induced to do it in the absence of any enemy or even any immediately obvious catastrophe. What will be required is a complete turnabout in our "way of life," **from one designed for conspicuous consumption,** stimulated via mass media advertising—so gratifying to the immediate profit motives of people in industry—**to one designed to maximize efficient and equitable utilization of the available resources of our planet.**

Pressures of Population and Development.   Probably the most important underlying problem of mankind is the pressure of an exponentially increasing population. The world population will theoretically reach 24 billion by the year 2075. Obviously, our planet's resources would not be able to support such a population.

As far as the "Have" nations are concerned, it is clear that the destruction of our ozone layer and our pollution of the environment is in no small part a function of the sheer numbers of people pushing the buttons, being kept warm in the winters and cool in the summers, and tossing their refuse around. And who can blame the "Have-not" countries for wanting what is called "development?" Within the past decade or so, there has been a sudden increase in demand for beef and pork. Producing meat is a **bad nutritional bargain,** because it takes about eight pounds of grain to make just one pound of meat. However, a shift in the dietary habits of affluent peoples in the "Have" countries would be resisted intensely by these people and would also be fought tooth and nail by the agriculture and food industries.

If increasing food supplies are *not* accompanied by birth control, **then population production will outrun food production by the Year 2000 at the latest**. Of course, procreation is a prime example of Immediate and Concrete Reinforcement—to which, in underdeveloped countries, is added the more Remote Symbolic Reinforcement of support in one's old age. The relative failure of the government in India to damp the national birth rate contrasts with the relative success in Mainland China, where strong community social pressures have been applied. As cruel as it may sound, transmission of food supplies from "Haves" to "Have-nots" may have to be made *contingent* upon efforts by the latter to damp their population growth.

Richard Lee Clinton (1977), claims that neither the capitalist nor the socialist approach to development will be successful as long as **industrialization** remains a leading strategy. The problems of population and development both relate to the struggle of the "Have-nots" to raise their **standard of living**—particularly since development in this sense has typically been accompanied by lower fertility rates—and **in an equitably balanced interdependent world** there would be no necessary correlation between standard of living and level of industrialization for individual countries (any more than there is for individual states of the U.S.).

THE PSYCHO-DYNAMICS OF ARMS RACES AND PEACE RACES

The psycho-dynamics of "uncalculated" escalation into arms races follow directly from the nature of Neanderthal thinking—and talking. Following the dictates of *Psycho-logic*, people easily turn the WE's into heroes and the THEY's into villians. Given his *Pollyannaism*—attempting to grasp onto the reassuring and push away the threatening aspects of his world—the Neanderthal mentality leads people to believe that "WE are falling behind

THEM in military strength" and, therefore, to support demands for more and more billions to guarantee that "WE are the strongest nation on earth!"

Given *Cognitive Stereotypy*, paradoxically, the more people's anxieties are increased by events—or, more often, by scare stories in the mass media—the more difficult the Neanderthal makes it to even comprehend any alternatives. And, since people are less influenced by *Reinforcements* that are *Remote and Symbolic* than by those that are *Immediate and Concrete*, they simply do not have the creative imagination to make immediate and concrete the horrors of nuclear catastrophes.

Arms Races

"Calculated" escalation—described by Herman Kahn (1965) as "a competition in resolve" and "a competition in risk-taking"—is a strategy that relies for its success upon Neanderthal thinking in high places as well as low. This strategy has three salient features: (a) the steps are *unilaterally initiated* (we did not negotiate with the North Vietnamese about increasing the tempo of our bombing or moving it closer to Hanoi); (b) each step propels the opponent into *reciprocating* if he can (our development of multiple nuclear warheads propels the Soviets into analogous developments); and (c) such steps are necessarily *graduated* in nature—by the unpredictability of technological breakthroughs, by the limitations imposed by logistics, and by the oscillating level of perceived threat.

Peace Races

But calculated escalation is obviously a *tension-increasing* process, the termination of which is a *military* resolution—victory, defeat, or even mutual annihilation. Now, if we change this last feature of calculated escalation—shift it from tension-induction to tension-reduction—we have the essence of *a calculated de-escalation strategy* in conflict situations. It is one in which nation A devises patterns of small steps, well within its own limits of security, designed to reduce tensions and induce reciprocating steps from nation B.

If such unilateral initiatives are persistently applied, and reciprocation is obtained, then the margin for risk-taking is widened and somewhat larger steps can be taken. Both sides, in effect, begin edging down the tension ladder, and both are moving—within what they perceive as reasonable limits of national security—toward a **political** rather than a military resolution. Successful application of such a strategy assumes that all parties to a conflict have strong motives to get out of it—which **should** be the case in this nuclear age.

The focus of my own long-term concern at the inter-nation level has been the rationalization of a strategy alternative whose technical name is *graduated and reciprocated initiatives in tension-reduction*. While doodling at a conference in the early 1960s, I realized that the initials of this mind-boggling phrase spelled GRIT—and, although I generally take a dim view of acronyms, this one was not only easy for people to remember but also suggested the kind of determination and patience required to apply it successfully.

Graduated and Reciprocated Initiatives in Tension-reduction (GRIT)

One of the aims of GRIT, a strategy alternative, is to reduce and control international tension levels. Another is to create an atmosphere of mutual trust within which negotiations on critical military and political issues can have a better chance of succeeding; in other words, GRIT is not a *substitute* for the more familiar process of negotiation, but rather a parallel process designed to enable a nation to take the *initiative* in a situation where a dangerous "balance" of mutual fear exists.

GRIT Strategy.   The GRIT strategy is unconventional and, therefore, open to suspicion abroad and resistance at home. Thus, it is necessary to spell out the *ground-rules* under which this particular "game" should be played. (See Osgood, 1977.)

Rules for Maintaining Security.   Rule 1: *Unilateral initiatives must not reduce one's capacity to inflict unacceptable nuclear retaliation should there be attack at that level*. Nuclear capacity can serve rational foreign policy (a), if it is viewed not only as a deterrent, but also as **a security base** from which to take limited risks in the direction of reducing tensions; (b), if the retaliatory, **second-strike nature** of the capacity is made explicit; and (c), if only **the minimum capacity** required for effective deterrence is maintained and the arms race damped.
Rule 2: *Unilateral initiatives must not cripple one's capacity to meet conventional aggression with appropriately graded conventional response*. Conventional forces must be maintained at rough parity in regions of confrontation. But the **absolute level** at which the balance is mainained is variable. The general rule would be to initiate unilateral moves in the regions of least tension and gradually extend them to what were originally the most tense regions.
Rule 3: *Unilateral initiatives must be graduated in risk according to the degree of reciprocation obtained from an opponent*. If bona fide reciprocations of appropriate magnitude are obtained, the magnitude and signifi-

cance of subsequent steps can be increased; if not, then the process continues with steps of about the same magnitude of risk. The *relative* risk thus remains roughly constant throughout the process.

Rule 4: *Unilateral initiatives should be diversified in nature, both as to sphere of action and as to geographical locus of application.* The reasons for diversification are two-fold: first, to minimize weakening one's position in any one sphere or geographical locus; second, to keep applying the pressure of initiatives **having a common tension-reducing intent,** but not "threatening" opponents by pushing steadily in the same sphere or locus, thereby limiting their options in reciprocating.

Rules for Inducing Reciprocation. Rule 5: *Unilateral initiatives must be designed and communicated so as to emphasize a sincere intent to reduce tensions.* Escalation and de-escalation strategies cannot be "mixed" in the military sense. The reason is psychological: reactions to **threats** are incompatible with reactions to **promises.**

Rule 6: *Unilateral initiatives should be publicly announced at some reasonable interval prior to their execution and identified as part of a deliberate policy of reducing tensions.* Prior announcements minimize the potentially unstabilizing effect of unilateral acts, and their identification with total GRIT strategy helps shape the opponent's interpretation of them. However, the GRIT process cannot **begin** with a large, precipitate, and potentially unstabilizing unilateral action.

Rule 7: *Unilateral initiatives should include in their announcement explicit invitation to reciprocation in some form.* The purpose of this "rule" is to increase pressure on an opponent—by making it clear that reciprocation of appropriate form and magnitude is essential to the momentum of GRIT— and to bring to bear pressures of world opinion. However, **exactly** specifying the form or magnitude or reciprocation has several drawbacks: having the tone of a demand, it carries an implied threat of retaliation if not met; furthermore, the specific reciprocation requested may be based on faulty perceptions of the other's situation. It is the occurrence of reciprocation *in any form,* yet having the same tension-reducing intent, that is critical. Psychologically, the greatest conciliatory impact upon opponents in a conflict situation is produced by their **voluntary reciprocation.** Such behavior is incompatible with opponents' Neanderthal beliefs about the unalterable hostility and aggressiveness of the initiator—and once opponents have reciprocated, all of the cognitive pressure is upon modifying these beliefs.

Rules for Demonstrating the Genuineness of Intent. Rule 8: *Unilateral initiatives that have been announced must be executed on schedule regardless of any prior commitments to reciprocate by the opponent.* This is the best indication of one's own intent to reduce tension. What and how much is committed is controlled by the graduated nature of the process. Failure to execute an announced step, however, would be a clear sign of ambivalence in intent. This is particularly important in the early stages, when announced initiatives are liable to the charge of "propaganda."

Rule 9: *Unilateral initiatives should be continued over a considerable period, regardless of the degree or even absence of reciprocation.* Like the steady pounding on a nail, pressure toward reciprocating builds up, as announced act follows announced act of a tension-reducing nature, even though the individual acts may be small in significance. The essence of this strategy *is* the calculated manipulation of *the intent component* of the perceived-threat-equals-capability-times-intent equation. It is always difficult to "read" the intentions of an opponent in a conflict situation, and they are usually very complex. In such a situation, GRIT can be applied consistently to encourage conciliatory intents and interpretations at the expense of aggressive ones.

Rule 10: *Unilateral initiatives must be as unambiguous and as susceptible to verification as possible.* Even overt deeds are liable to misinterpretation. Inviting opponent verification via direct, on-the-spot observation or via indirect media observation (e.g., televising the act in question), along with requesting verification of reciprocal actions, is ideal—and what little might be *lost* in the way of secrecy by both sides may be more than made up by a *reduced need* for secrecy on both sides.

ONE WORLD OR NO WORLD

Science and technology will not solve all our problems. We must somehow meet the Russell-Einstein challenge by trying to create a massive change in **our** *ways of thinking:* We must change our ways of thinking *about* the objective problems. We must also try to *buy more time*—time to allow people in decision-making positions to *think,* rather than simply *react habitually* to the day-to-day crises. The GRIT strategy is one way of doing this.

A basic issue is *Ego-ism* vs. *Alter-ism* in the conduct of human affairs. *Ego-ism* is simply the flowering of Darwinian dynamics of evolution—*survival* (power and profit) *of the fittest*—into an age when one species, humanoid primates, dominates the earth. Yet, most interestingly, it is this species that—not innately like the ant, but adaptively through learning—has found that Ego-ism *can* be satisfied within Alter-istic social structures. Quite simply, *Alter-ism* is putting the welfare of others above the welfare of the self—with the realization that, in the long run, one's own welfare is intimately tied to that of others.

Individuals who are profiteering in the proliferation of nuclear capabilities might realize that their own lives and those of their loved ones are just as "probablistic" as the lives of all the faceless unknowns. Nucler weapons do not play favorites.

The Free Enterprise System—which really isn't very "free" anymore—is essentially Ego-istic. What we have been moving into rapidly, even if imperceptibly, is what can fairly be called "The New Slavery": More than half of all the personal wealth in the U.S., for example, is now owned (and controlled) by only 6 percent of the population.

The most glaring inconsistency of our time is that we are already living in a highly *interdependent* world and yet are trying to run it politically with competing "ego-istic" national governments. A prime example of intolerance of ambiguity in the semantics of international politics is the reification of *nations* as the prime units in international affairs. Part of any semantic revolution must be an *increase* in the ambiguity of nation-names, by using language which deliberately levels distinctions *between* nations and sharpens differences *within* them. This implies gradual dissolution of the nation-state as the prime political unit.

Given the degree of interdependence that already exists on this planet—not only in the production of nuclear materials (proliferation) and their potential use, but also in the world economy (multinational corporate control over the flow of resources), in the effects upon the environment (pollution of the air and the oceans), and even in communications (computerization and satellites)—we have already reached the point in human history where it *is* functionally One World. But where the essentials of human existence are involved—energy, food, transportation, and, indeed, life itself—control is in the hands of individuals and not society as a whole.

REFERENCES

CARTER, L.J. (1977). The radioactive waste inventory. *Science 195*, 662.

CLINTON, R.L. (1977). The never-to-be developed countries of Latin America. *Bulletin of the Atomic Scientists*. (Oct.), 19-26.

FRANK, J. (1977). "Some Psychological Aspects of the Proliferation of Nuclear Power." (Paper distributed at the 27th Pugwash Conference, Munich, West Germany.)

KAHN, H. (1965). "On Escalation: Metaphors and Scenarios." New York: Praeger.

OSGOOD, C.E. (1971). Conservative words and radical sentences in the semantics of international politics. *In* G. Abcarian and J.W. Soule (Eds.), "Social Psychology and Political Behavior," pp. 100-129. Columbus, OH: Merill.

OSGOOD, C.E. (1977). "GRIT for MBFR: A Proposal for Unfreezing Force Level Postures in Europe." (Paper for 27th Pugwash Confrence, Munich, West Germany.)

SUEDFELD, P., TETLOCK, P.E., and RAMIREZ, C. (1977). War, peace and integrative complexity. *Journal of Conflict Resolution 21*, 427-441.

WALD, G. (1975). There isn't much time. *The Progressive* (Dec.), 22-24.

PART **IV**

METHOD IN
CULTURE STUDY

15

Intercultural Communication Research:
A Burke's Eye View

TRICIA S. JONES
Ohio State University
Athens, Ohio 45701

The past two decades have witnessed the addition of a new member to the family of communication study. Although it remains quintessentially adolescent, intercultural communication has evolved from an adopted offspring obtained from sociology and anthropology to a legitimate fixture in the field of communication (Samovar and Porter, 1972). However, communication scholars have yet to imprint this new member with the traditions of their 2,000-year-old patriarch, rhetoric.

Some attempts to intertwine the field of rhetoric and its new consort have been attempted. Blake (1979) succinctly summarized the current state of affairs when he reported that there is no significant body of knowledge that treats the subjects of rhetoric and intercultural communication. In an effort to rectify this apparent oversight, this paper attempts to utilize Burke's key constructs of rhetorical theory as a method of justifying, directing, and utilizing intercultural communication research. The application of Burke's concepts is preceded by a brief explication of the purposes of intercultural communication research and the prominent methods used to conduct that research.

Intercultural communication research serves three general purposes. It describes the nature of communication in specific cultures, highlighting the differences and similarities between cultures. Based upon this knowledge, researchers can study ways to erase the communication differences that act as barriers between members of different cultures. Researchers concerned primarily with the study of differences belong to the cultural criticism school of research (Asante et al., 1979). Conversely, researchers may emphasize the similarities of cultures in order to generate a more holistic conception of human communication; such researchers and theorists are considered cultural dialoguists (Asante et al., 1979). Finally, the culmination of this research serves as a foundation for obtaining a better understanding of our culture, and the creation and ramifications of culture in general.

The roots of intercultural communication research are buried deep within the disciplines of sociology and anthropology, and to a lesser extent, psychology. Not surprisingly, the major branches of intercultural communication research are typified by the use of three methodologies more commonly found in the scholarly works of these fields rather than in communication. These methodologies—cultural variable analysis, componential analysis, and ethnomethodology—have contributed the majority of information in this area (Burk and Lukens, 1979).

Cultural variable analysis is the empirical examination of single or multiple variables of cultural behavior. Although the field of communication is no stranger to empiricism, it was not its creator or validator. Communicationists borrowed the empirical hammer from its neighbor, psychology. Communication researchers have pounded at intercultural variables with the same bicep-building determination that characterizes many other areas of communication research (Becker, 1969). Cultural variable analysis focuses on the different value systems underlying cultural activities. Its proponents and practitioners are usually cultural critics seeking to illuminate differences between cultures.

The praises of deterministic research have been sung by many, and its inadequacies have been pronounced by more than a few. Empiricism in this context deserves some specific criticism. Cultural variable analysts often research isolated variables, thereby removing them from the cultural context which gives them meaning. The selection of suitable variables is rarely predicated upon a thorough knowledge of the culture, which is probably necessary before "important" variables can be recognized (Burk and Lukens, 1979; Chu, 1964). All too often this research is ethnocentrically focused on Western societies and on how members of non-Western societies react in Western culture.

Cognitive anthropolgy was devleoped to obtain insight into the cognitive realities of a society's members. Goodenough (1960) suggested that cultures are composed of psychological structures which guide behavior. Therefore, cognitive anthropologists believe that these structures can be analyzed by formal methods similar to those used in mathematics and logic (Geertz, 1973). The primary tool used in this analysis (a different kind of hammer) is componential analysis, which attempts to establish a relationship between categories of language and objects, concepts, or events. By discovering these relationships, theorists supposedly can construct a formal model of how people use terminology to reflect their social reality. Moreover, once constructed, this model can be applied regardless of the idiosyncracies of the studied culture.

As with cultural variable analysis, componential analysis suffers specific shortcomings. The quasi-laws approach, coupled with the stated goal of an acultural formal calculus, removes the possibility, indeed the intention, of considering the creation of meaning. Componential analysis is highly restrictive, concerning itself only with verbal language. Interestingly, even with the emphasis on linguistics; most, if not all, cognitive anthropologists are not concerned with the biases and assumptions that their own language dictates.

Spawned from modern sociology, ethnomethodology studies how people make decisions and create meaning in everyday life (Garfinkel, 1960). The benefit of ethnomethodology lies in the discovery of social constructions of reality. Drawing mainly upon phenomenological assumptions, ethnomethodologists study the totality of behavior, verbal and nonverbal. More importantly, it is not enough to record a behavior, it is essential to understand the meaning that a behavior has for a member of that society (Psathas, 1972). The information gathered by ethnomethodology is dependent upon social placement and historical meaning due to the reliance of a culture's members on background expectations in interpreting actions (Garfinkel, 1960).

"Thick description" is the term Geertz (1973) uses to identify the recording of information in an ethnographic study. Quite simply, to describe something "thickly" necessitates observing a behavior and explicating the meaning of that behavior (Sanday, 1979). Thick description is microscopic and more intuitive than cultural variable analysis or componential analysis. Unfortunately, it is also more difficult to establish the validity of thick description. Even so, thick description can be used to construct theories of intercultural communication, although these theories will be culturally bound and therefore rules- rather than laws-oriented (Geertz, 1973).

All three methods of intercultural communication research are subject to criticism; yet, all are potentially informative. It is apparent that each method requires the researcher to adopt certain assumptions. The contrasting assumptions implicit in these three methods raise questions concerning general criteria for acceptable intercultural communication research. Generally, it is safe to assume that valid and informative intercultural research depends on at least the following three criteria. (a), Researchers should understand the studied culture thoroughly enough to recognize salient variables (Psathas, 1972). (b), Researchers should be aware of the world-view assumptions that they adopt, and the effects these assumptions have on their research. (c), Finally, the ultimate focus of research should be on the accurate portrayal of the meaning and function of communicative behavior (Geertz, 1973).

At this point it might seem that something is missing. Where is the communication theory underlying intercultural communication research? Briefly, it isn't there. By borrowing methods from other disciplines, communicationists have borrowed theoretical assumptions as well; or worse, have sidestepped the question of theory altogether (Samovar and Porter, 1972).

The remainder of this paper proposes and justifies the efficacy of Burke's rhetorical theory as a much needed basis for intercultural communication research. Burke's definition of rhetoric guides intercultural communication researchers in the selection of variables and/or objects of study. Broadening the view of rhetoric proposed by the classical rhetoricians, Burke suggests that persuasion is synonymous with rhetoric, and that persuasion exists wherever there is meaning (Golden et al., 1976). This definition of rhetoric is similar to Ehninger's definition that rhetoric is "All of the ways in which, and all of the ends for which, symbols of any sort may be used to influence or affect another's mind" (Blake, 1979; p. 87).

The significance of Burke's definition of rhetoric is that it suggests that any meaningful activity comprises rhetoric and therefore should be considered in an analysis of communicative behavior. Furthermore, Burke's "rhetoric" implies specific guidelines for the selection of heuristic cultural variables. First, the synonymity of meaningful behavior and rhetoric stipulates that the process of meaning creation cannot be divorced from intercultural communication research. This signals the necessity of viewing intercultural communication in its natural context. Second, although the study of language is informative and necessary, it is not enough. A culture's activities such as music, dance, art, and rituals are meaningful and therefore rhetorical. In this sense, the cognitive anthropologists are blinded to alternative objects of examination by their limited reliance on linguistic analysis. Similarly, cultural variable analysts ascribe meaning to outcomes, yet fail to establish the justification of their ascriptions from the subject's view of reality.

The aforestated definition of rhetoric provides clues to methodologies that can be profitably employed in intercultural communication research, due to its inclusion within Burke's dramatistic perspective. For Burke, dramatism is "a technique of anlaysis of language and thought as basically modes of action rather than as a means of conveying information" (Burke, 1968, p. 53). The emphasis on action portrays human behavior as motivated, or as creating meaning and being assigned meaning, through the completion of activity. Human motives, specifically grammatical motives, concern the problem of substance. Burke's explanation of substance bridges the chasm between individual acts and the resultant social order. As Nichols stated:

> According to Burke, language of all things "is most public, most collective, in its substance." Substance in the old philosophies was an act, and a way of life an acting together; and in acting together men have common sensations, concepts, images, ideas, and attitudes that make them consubstantial. (Golden et al., 1976, p. 239)

The dramatistic world view paints man as creating reality through meaningful activity. Although Burke singles out language in this explanation of the substantive meaning of dramatism, it is not congruent with his definition of rhetoric to limit theorists and researchers to linguistic studies. The construction of reality is a process in which shared symbols "both fit and adjust behavior to a symbolically created world" (Golden et al., 1976, p. 240). Burke's world view corresponds to a predominantly sociological orientation. His conception of motivation contrasts with the conception of motivation in the physical sciences, i.e., that motivation may be considered in mechanistic terms of cause and effect (Nichols, 1952). Burke's motivation is explanatory rather than prescriptive.

What are the methodological consequences of the dramatistic perspective? This perspective emphasizes the active process of meaning creation and human motivation. Therefore, it is essential for rhetoricians, researchers, or communicationists to study communication as a process. Furthermore, communication cannot be dissected and displaced to increase the convenience of observation without disrupting the process of meaning creation. Adjunctly, behavior cannot or should not be separated from the cultural context which supplies meaning. Ascertaining the motivations of an actor seems to necessitate the use of reflexive interrogation by the actor and the researcher. Reflexive determination allows determination of motives by reviewing completed action. In short, the dramatistic perspective requires research that examines meaning creation as a culturally bound process validated by reflexive inquiry.

The dramatistic perspective limits the utility of cultural variable analysis and componential analysis as these methods are practised today. Cultural variable analysis violates this perspective by disrupting the process of communication through isolation of variables. The isolation of variables assumes linear determinism and ignores the importance of cultural contexts.

Componential analysis, although not quite as inappropriate as the former method, restricts researchers from analyzing many types of meaningful behavior because it focuses on language as the cognitive key. It ignores the role of language as created meaning and eschews reflexive validation by the informants.

Ethnomethodology appears most congruent with the dramatistic perspective. Focusing on the process of meaning creation in the totality of human behavior reinforces the importance of the cultural contexts. Ethnomethodology is limited mainly by the willingness of the researchers to utilize reflexive validation techniques. The paradigm itself does not impose this restriction; researchers merely prefer to validate their findings by comparing them with findings of other scholars.

In the dramatistic perspective a key concept is terministic screens. This element suggests a "Weltanschauungen" assumption of the world view that researchers bring to their endeavors and that societal members operate within. Terministic screens are perceptual filters that are a product of the suasive nature of language. These filters direct the selection of stimulus and the interpretation of stimulus. As Burke (1968, p. 44) stated, "If terminology is a reflection of reality, by its very nature it is a selection of reality and therefore also functions as a deflection of reality."

As an interesting parallel to the schools of cultural criticism and cultural dialogue, Burke suggests that there are basically two kinds of terms and corresponding screens: those that put things together, and those that take things apart (Burke, 1968). Extending this parallel indicates that psychology's focus on individuality yields a "difference-oriented" perspective, while anthropology's and sociology's focus on social characteristics depends on an "integrative" perspective. Therefore, terministic screens can function similarly to the paradigmatic filters discussed by Kuhn (1962).

Different scholarly disciplines possess terministic screens which are designed to "focus attention on one or another particular field of observation" (Burke, 1968, p. 52). The profundity of this statement is readily apparent in a review of the three methods of intercultural communication research. Cultural variable analysis flows from psychology, componential analysis from anthropology, and ethnomethodology from sociology. Cultural variable analysis investigates individual differences while componential analysis and ethnomethodology study binding social activities. Both ethnomethodology and the dramatistic perspective are inherently sociological; therefore it reasonably follows that the sociological methodology most accurately captures the essence of the dramatistic view.

The overriding significance of terministic screens is that they render it impossible for one discipline to to "supply an adequate definition of man in general" (Burke, 1968, p. 58). Yet the dramatistic screen does possess the philosophic character necessary for the discussion of man in general (Burke, 1968).

The effects of researchers' terministic screens present the possibility, more accurately the probability, that researchers' selections and interpretations of intercultural communication data is biased. This realization requires researchers to recognize their operating screens and to act against biased selection and interpretation activities. Two methods might prove helpful in safeguarding the objectivity and validity of research findings. First, researchers should become familiar with other approaches to intercultural research, thereby escaping the restrictions of the screens operating in their disciplines. Second, self-reflexiveness of informants and reactions of scholars from other disciplines could provide validation checks on the original interpretation.

The dramatistic perspective constructs an image of communication as sociality. Sociality derives its essence from the synchronization and fusion of unique individuals typified by divisiveness. All people exist in a state of generic division which increases at a societal or class level (Nichols, 1952). Subsequently, when people from different classes or societies communicate, an aura of mystery signifies the interaction, creating barriers that inhibit sharing and understanding. This is the distinguishing characteristic of intercultural communication.

Burke stresses that "the mystery which exists between classes demands a corresponding rhetoric" (Fry, 1980). This rhetoric is typified by the process of identification in which someone or some group attempts to transcend the innate differences between them and the people they communicate with. Identification has been heralded as the key term in Burke's rhetorical theory, replacing the reversed position of persuasion in classical theories (Ambrester, 1974). Instead of manipulating an audience, identification involves understanding the use of symbols as masks for the differences between peoples and directing attentions toward the use of those symbols to overcome communication barriers (Fry, 1980). Therefore, the function of identification is found in its complementarity with division. "If men were not apart from one another there would be no need for the rhetorician to proclaim their unity" (Burke, 1969, p. 115). As such, identification leads to understanding which in turn may evolve into cooperation.

The theoretical elements presented in the dramatistic perspective are completed and conjoined through the process of identification. Likewise, the process of intercultural communication research culminates with identification. It suggests the purpose of such research; specifically, overcoming the barriers between cultures and creating an opportunity of spreading the basis of the social order by fusing social factions.

Applying Burke's rhetorical theories to intercultural communication does more than justify the inclusion of this area in the rubric of communication studies. Hopefully, Burke's theories justify the selection of intercultural variables, implicate appropriate methodologies, instruct researchers about possibly invalidating biases, and explicate methods to use research findings. Burke's emphasis on meaning mandates observation of all meaningful behavior. The dramatistic perspective relegates cultural variable analysis and componential analysis to the status of inferior research methodologies compared with ethnomethodology. Researchers using sociological methods may improve the validity of their interpretations by recognizing the effects of their terministic screens. Finally, researchers, practioners, and cultural members may utilize the recognition of differences and construct bonds that identify commonalities and eliminate differences. Under the tutelage of old man rhetoric, intercultural communication may successfully pass from adolescence to adulthood.

REFERENCES

AMBRESTER, R. (1974). Identification within; Kenneth Burke's view of the unconscious. *Philosophy and Rhetoric 7*, 205-215.

ASANTE, M.K., NEWMARK, E., and BLAKE, C.A. (1979). The field of intercultural communication. *In* M.K. Asante, E. Newmark, and C.A. Blake (Eds.), "Handbook of Intercultural Communication," pp. 11-22. Beverley Hills, CA: Sage.

BECKER, S.L. (1969). Directions for intercultural communication research. *Central States Speech Journal 20*, 3-13.

BLAKE, C.A. (1979). Rhetoric and intercultural communication. *In* M.K. Asante, E. Newmark, and C.A. Blake (Eds.), "Handbook of Intercultural Communication," pp. 84-94. Beverly Hills, CA: Sage.

BURK, J., and LUKENS, J.G. (1979). On the relevance of cognitive anthropology and ethnomethodology. *In* M.K. Asante, E. Newmark, and C.A. Blake (Eds.), "Handbook of Intercultural Communication," pp. 43-56. Beverly Hills, CA: Sage.

BURKE, K. (1968). "Language as Symbolic Action; Essays on Life, Literature, and Method." Berkeley, CA: University of California Press.

BURKE, K. (1969). "The Rhetoric of Motives." Berkeley, CA: University of California Press.

CHU, G.C. (1964). Problems of cross-cultural communication research. *Journalism Quarterly 47*, 557-562.

FRY, V. (1980). "Heads I Win—Tails You Lose: A Preliminary Analysis of Kenneth Burke's Concept of Mystery." (Paper presented at the Speech Communication Association Convention, New York.)

GARFINKEL, H. (1969). "Studies in Ethnomethodology." Englewood Cliffs, NJ: Prentice-Hall.

GEERTZ, C. (1973). "The Interpretation of Cultures." New York: Basic Books.

GOLDEN, J.L., BERQUIST, G.F., and COLEMAN, W.E. (1976). "The Rhetoric of Western Thought." 2nd ed., Dubuque, IA: Kendall-Hunt.

GOODENOUGH, W. (1970). "Description and Comparison in Cognitive Anthropology." Chicago, IL: Aldine.

KUHN, T. (1962). "The Structure of Scientific Revolutions." Chicago, IL: University of Chicago Press.

NICHOLS, M.H. (1952). Kenneth Burke and the "new rhetoric." *Quarterly Journal of Speech 38*, 133-144.

PSATHAS, G. (1972). Ethnoscience and ethnomethodology. *In* J. Spradley (Ed.), "Culture and Cognition," pp. 206-222. San Francisco, CA: Chandler.

SAMOVAR, L.A., and PORTER, R.E. (Eds.) (1972). "Intercultural Communication." Belmont, CA: Wadsworth.

SANDAY, P.R. (1979). The ethnographic paradigm(s). *Administrative Science Quarterly 24*, 527-538.

16

Method and Meaning in Anthropology; A Discussion of Language*

DIANNE ASHTON
Temple University
Philadelphia, Pennsylvania 19122

In the social sciences, trust in a science-like method was a reaction to traditional religious assertions on the nature of humanity and of revelation as the primary source of truth. Descartes' philosophy was the base. But Descartes wrote that truth could be reached through observation of things as they are, precisely because God is a good judge, and that the world bears witness to His power. He saw the human capacity to know both God and matter explained in the dual nature of human life itself. His famous mind-body schism was the solution that could allow science its place in the concerns of matter, while retaining a God of the spirit. This brilliant solution secured the position of natural scientists for centuries to come.

But social scientists have run into trouble. It is not just that participant observation is a contradiction in terms, but, as Mbiti (1969) suggests, that anthropologists have frequently been plain wrong about other religions. The meaning of a religion was often either deduced from a formal analysis of the relationship of its symbols, or just intuited by the researcher. Often projections distorted everyone's views. This inability to deal effectively with religion is the result of a more fundamental difficulty in dealing with questions of meaning.

Martin Heidegger's analysis of Descartes' work can give us a key to understanding the root of this problem in anthropology. Further, his presentation of a thematic examination of the meaning of Being indicates ways for possible improvement. This paper first examines the work of Heidegger

---

*With special thanks to Dr. Thomas Dean, Religion Department, Temple University.

and Descartes in its relationship to anthropological concerns and then turns to a work by Michelle Rosaldo which illustrates what a Heidegger-based anthropology would look like. In light of these themes, the paper considers whether or not traditionally nonliterate, small societies can be considered more stable than large, modern societies.

By looking at Being-in-the-world, at existence as known by the existing being, Heidegger develops a reservoir of coherent understanding from which we may draw. He eliminates the chasms between Wittgenstein's ill-defined "forms of life," and presents a unified, single process of Being. Quite simply, he makes Being a verb, and by implication, human being is a species of actions. Primary among the actions of this species is the use of language, which permeates all understanding. He compares the discourse of two natural languages, modern German and pre-Socratic Greek, to philosophical technical language in developing his own work on meaning, *Being and Time* (Heidegger, 1962).

Heidegger points out that Descartes' approach took its lead from the description of things. In this, the object remains undisturbed and unaffected. People are treated as a type of thing, thinking thing. Heidegger takes issue with both the initial assumption and the process of argument. He points out that, because the issue of meaning, not just thought, is fundamental to human nature, we cannot say we understand people if we do not understand what they mean by being. For people, being-in-the-world is irreducible. Our existence is permeated with an understanding of its meaning. This understanding is not static, but shaped by our growth and experience within our societies. There is no meaninglessness prior to our experience as people. Individuation is a process resulting from, among other things, our anxiety over our own death. Since there is no normal human life apart from this process of understanding, it is fruitless and inadequate to study humans without attention to this dimension.

The question is, of course, how are we to study meaning? Heidegger and Michelle Rosaldo suggest a plan. Heidegger insists that Being is always the being of an entity. The best method for studying this is *not* a logical analysis of cause and effect among its particular attributes, but a carefully travelled hermeneutic circle of investigation. This can reveal whole phenomena, like meaning, because in this process we are always confronting and readjusting previous partial understandings in the creation of something more complete and genuine. Projection can be considered one arc of the circle, so to speak, to be extended and integrated into any thorough investigation. Truth, then, for Heidegger, is not merely the coherence of argument, nor the collection of attributes to build ever more complex descriptions of a relatively unaffected reality "out there," but the uncovering of phenomena as they exist in presenting themselves to us. Encounter is the fundamental concept.

This may seem a conflation of the ontic and ontological levels, a distinction Heidegger is careful to maintain. Instead of "humans," he speaks of Dasein, that being for whom its being is an issue. There are any number of reasons why he decided to use Dasein: to focus on the active process of existing that is always already in a context not of its own making (thrown), to avoid conceptual traps regarding "consciousness," or to keep himself out of debates over the nature of a range of beings, animal to theological. The consistent focus of his work in *Being and Time* is the meaning of Being for Dasein, written by Dasein. It is a single question encompassing the whole of existence. In this, the ontic is in interaction with the ontological. They are not philosophical constructs, but occurrences within the fabric of Dasein's existence. As such, while they may not always be harmoniously supportive, neither can they "fly in the face of" each other. It may be debated whether or not beings other than humans are Dasein; however, Dasein is at least human.

This has direct implications for research in anthropology. Instead of learning a people's language in order to converse about other things, we see the importance of discovering the culture within the language and conversations themselves. The method for studying beings and the method for studying the meaning of Being are brought into the same field of exploration. In this light, we see that participant observation is not an exercize in which conclusions are proved. It is an exploration. The researcher is not a disembodied intellect, but a person meeting other people. Everyone brings the meaning of his/her life to the encounter. In addition to everything else, we need to consider local history and custom in affecting what people choose to tell us about themselves, as well as the affect of our own histories on our understanding of them. The point of this perspective is not to improve our chances of getting closer to the "objective facts," but to allow human reality to more intelligently enter our reports. Heidegger speaks of digging away at the debris of misunderstanding so that the truth can let itself be revealed. Michelle Rosaldo seems to illustrate this idea in *Knowledge and Passion* (1980), her book on the Ilongot, a head-hunting people in the Philippines.

While she credits Wittgenstein with the inspiration to attend to language, her route is more like Heidegger's. She includes material on environment, economy, family relationships, political organization, and cosmology, digging away at the debris of our total ignorance. But this only sets the stage for her discussion of meaning for the Ilongot. She supports her approach with an argument that echoes Heidegger's. She says that the effort to reach understanding through "objective" description has led to a division of language into two parts; words that seem to have a literal meaning, that is, can be understood by reference to an external, thing-like referant, and words with "symbolic" meanings. This has been motivated either by the philosophical position or the emotional impulse that beneath our cultural differences lies a human essence which can be understood as easily as a common sense understanding of our next door neighbors. Whatever remains incomprehensible, or unavailable to common sense understanding, is consigned to the symbolic, i.e., religious. Under this new heading it is again subject to the same sort of dissection by reference. What is left is often put to strictly logical analysis. In this way, symbolic becomes a catch word for obscurity.

By cutting up language into the easily understood and the exotically obscure, anthropologists also cut up their hosts' world according to foreign categories. As Rosaldo, Geertz (1975) and Goffman (1974) insist, it is the everyday, that which we tend to take at face value, which requires an interpretive account, so that the meaning of the whole of life is revealed. For this, attention needs be paid not only to words, but nuances, idioms, phrases, contexts, gestures, tones, and dress. With this approach, religion has a better chance of emerging with its potential for inspiration intact. No living religion is ever divorced from the truth of a people's life, and it is this truth that is its meaning.

Rosaldo goes after issues of meaning in Ilongot life directly, sidestepping the problems many educated westerners have with religion per se, by focusing specifically on ontology. She found the primary tensions in Ilongot life and their drama in social, family, individual, and ontological forms. She writes:

> The two terms that are the subject of my text—beya and liget—knowledge and passion—capture well this tension between civility and unrestrained vitality, bespeaking the dependence of cooperative life and reasoned activity upon potentially disruptive force. These words are among the most significant in Ilongot talk of social life and feeling; they are related not as "cultural" rule to human "nature," but instead as complementary aspects of life in a society in which both civility and violence are understood with reference to the motions of the individual heart. (Rosaldo, 1980, p. 44)

Rosaldo's work on the Ilongot and Heidegger's *Being and Time* show that serious examination of the language with which a people speaks of itself can reveal complexities of meaning. Consistent with his training as a philosopher in Germany in the 1900s, Heidegger is more sensitive to historical then to cultural differences. He insists that any understanding of life is always within an understanding of the meaning of both history and time.

This is a provocative idea for anthropologists dealing with comparative rates of change. I would like to use the ideas discussed earlier to look at the widespread assumption that small, face-to-face cultures are more stable than large, modern societies. First, is there any reason to asusme that this refers to anything that can be called a fact? Are there fewer widespread cultural changes within an equally measured time span in small societies than in large? There seems to be no evidence for this assertion. Let us use for our time frame the last 180 years, and technological change as our lever.

As rapid as technological change has been in large modern societies, it cannot be compared for impact to the scope of such changes in small, traditional societies. If we use as our model for large modern societies western Europe and the United States, we must conclude that while standards and methods of mobility, leisure, and working conditions have changed, bringing with them changes in the economic strength of families that have altered the importance of family relationships, these have all occurred within a larger organizational framework that has remained sufficiently secure to keep national identity and, by and large, national boundaries and larger political relationships intact. By contrast, technological change in small traditional societies has had a far more profound impact, dramatically affecting political organization, family, life, religion, and mode of work. Certainly, we cannot ignore the fact that most of the technological changes have come from developments within the modern societies themselves, and so have been better incorporated into national life, as the people have a context of meaning into which such changes may fit. The technological change of the last 180 years in small, traditional cultures has, by and large, come through the harsh channels of earlier colonization, forced conversion, and deliberate manipulation and destruction of the authority of tradition. When colonists were overthrown, governments and national boundaries set up by the indigenous population had lost their traditional structure. Traditional forces of social control either remained lost or were much reduced in strength. This was true even where attempts at revitalization of the traditional culture were made, since now it was a voluntary association, an ethnicity.

This brief history does not indicate that small societies are better able to withstand change than large. Nor, however, does it tell us anything about how they deal with change developed from within. Where could this idea have come from? Perhaps from problems in the condition of field work itself.

It is hardly necessary to remind ourselves that many early anthropologists thought they were looking at living fossils. Because their hosts had developed neither the technology of Europe nor its intellectual sophistication, small traditional societies were seen as lost in time. We know now that the technology of most small societies was designed to maintain a balance of nature rather than reach dominion over it. In all cultures, intellectual sophistication only begins with a thorough knowledge of language and tradition. It often stays beyond the researcher's grasp.

Further, we should not ignore the anthropologist's existential condition. It seems likely that he/she feels the tension of modern society most acutely. The frequent travelling of field workers, the rootlessness and solitary life demanded by advanced academic training, no doubt contribute to this. The lonely problem of adjusting to life in the host society, while refraining from "going native," add their share. Perhaps the desire to find a stable tradition is projected onto their work. An objective study dividing the world into the everyday-literal and the inscrutable-symbolic does not help us cope with this projection. Heidegger's (1962), and later, Gadamer's (1975) model of a hermeneutic circle of investigation in which language is left whole and projection an expected and useful arc, does.

Yet, the anthropologist does have data, and often their hosts report that the reason that some practice is done in a particular way is that it has "always" been done so. How are we to understand this "always"? Rosaldo describes an encounter with an Ilongot woman raising a family in the midst of practices derived from both traditional religion and Christianity. During the conversation, the Ilongot woman consigned a recently abandoned custom to the distant past. Because Rosaldo lets us know that the woman spoke nostalgically of an idealized past, the woman becomes real to us. We see that giving a new custom the stature of tradition may ease the strain of transition, painting the new as stable and reliable.

It seems clear that this depth of understanding will remain inaccessible if we continue to divide language and meaning into the objectively true and the symbolically illusory. If anthropology can teach us anything, it is to admit the complexity of human life. So far, it seems that the best route to understanding the complex whole of another's existence begins by acknowledging the subtlety, dimension, and power of language for all of us.

REFERENCES

GADAMER, H.-G. (1975). "Truth and Method." New York: Seabury Press.

GEERTZ, C. (1975). Common sense as a cultural system. *Antioch Review* 3 (No. 1), 5-26.

GOFFMAN, E. (1974). "Frame Analysis; An Essay on the Organization of Experience." New York: Harper Colophon Books.

HEIDEGGER, M. (1962). "Being and Time." Trans. by J. Macquarrie and E. Robinson. New York: Harper and Row.

MBITI, J.S. (1969). "African Religions and Philosophy." New York: Anchor Books.

17

Visual Anthropology's Contribution to Behavioral
Science with Observations on Why Anthropology
Appears to Turn Away from Nonverbal Evidence

JOHN COLLIER, JR.
San Francisco State University
San Francisco, California 94132

This paper reviews photography's contribution to anthropology, and discusses
social science's reluctance to use nonverbal data in its research. The disciplines that give anthropology its integrity are also its limitations in describing
the whole view, for the rigors of method necessarily sacrifice much descriptive
refinement. Hence, the view of anthropology is as limited as the character
of its data, which is generally demographic statistical information and ver-
batim interview statements of the native consultant. By default, the scientific
record often presents a gross image of the cultures studied.

Possibly this is a 19th century view, but regardless of the evolution of
field methods, anthropology today is limited by the tangibility of its data.
Most field procedures are directed to gathering tangible information unaffected by the impressionism or bias of the observer. Data must be "clean"—
free of all subjectivity. This ethos of authenticity comes from the laboratory
sciences, where this character of evidence is practical. But in anthropology,
"clean data" may not be realistically possible, for much information is gathered
over a bridge of human relations established by the rapport (projectivity) of
the field worker. Because of this circumstance, observers severely repress
their "feelings," the very perceptions which allow the artist-writer to present
the nuances and refinements of personality and culture which are usually
missing from ethnographic description. Admirably, the authentic source of
information is the native's view, from within, that is gathered through interviewing. Anything the consultant says is tangible and "clean information."
Disciplined field notes, transcribed not to reflect the investigator's feelings,
gather inventories of cultural behavior that report what happens reliably,
but rarely *how* actions happen. Modern research is more concerned with

why and *how* than, factually, what happens, but anthropology has no direct way of gathering this expansion of significance except by asking; hence, descriptively, this refinement may not be found in the data file.

The major contribution of visual anthropology is to broaden the scope of tangible information, so that refinements of literary description can be expressed in the anthropological record. Thus, visual anthropology is based on the photographic record that can reflect those human refinements that are beyond the content of the field notebook. Of course, much of this description could be gathered by simple direct observation, but this would require making value judgements that could be projectively misleading. Without photography, there is no objective way to make qualifying observations; so it is reasonable that, historically, anthropology has been a verbal discipline. As an example, Franz Boas enforced the discipline of learning native languages, so that indigenes could authentically share their ways verbally with the field worker.

The question is, "how comprehensive and supportive is interview data?" At Cornell University, graduate students were assigned to the raw data files of the Stirling County research project so they might describe a Stirling man and woman accurately. In the final seminar, each student presented a sketch but none of the descriptions satisfied those who knew the people, because nuance and descriptive refinement were missing from the raw data files.

Many of the overtones so necessary to the art of human description are tangible in photographic content. This photographic intelligence is indispensable to geography, archeology, and psychiatry. All of these fields exploit the orientation and mapping abilities of the camera record.

Photographs are more than information. In anthropology, they are artifacts and can be directly studied through a variety of analyses. The camera is also a measuring and counting tool that maps spacial relationships precisely. The camera can record vast inventories of cultural items that can then be studied directly and categorized within photographs. The camera can also track behavior through time and space (film).

My first experiment in using photography in behavioral research was made as part of a study of Acadian French and English response to rapid technological change. In collaboration, I designed and photographed a visual interview experiment that probed how French Acadian farmers responded to working in English industry.[1] This was the initial experiment in using photographs as artifacts to elicit feelings and gain facts dealing with a research circumstance. How to read information responsibly in photographs was mastered partially by our consultants reading this data for us. This experience was the first methodological effort to see through "native eyes," through their interpretations of photographs. Robert Smith, now an eminent scholar

---

[1] Alexander Leighton, his students, and colleagues were of great support.

of Japanese culture, used an old map to extend interview sessions and to stimulate the memory of informants, who said after one meeting, "Bob, I already told you all I know!"

I assembled an interview file covering the migration of Acadian French farmers into the English industries of Bristol. With the collaboration of the field workers, I carried out an experiment to test the value of interviewing with photographic probes. One field worker interviewed with verbal probes only, and a second field worker interviewed with structured photographs of French migration into the English industrial community.

In contrasting results, the field worker interviewing with verbal probes was able to complete only one and one-half interrogations, whereas the interviewer probing with photographs was able to interrogate indefinitely as long as he continued to bring in structured photographs. The photographic probes polarized and structured the interviews around the project's inquiry. Non-photographic interviewing drifted in content and, after one interview, began losing momentum. With photographic stimuli, the second and third interviews were as rewarding as the first (Collier, 1957).

Later, other investigators in various fields have used photographs and drawings as stimuli in projective interviewing. Spindler used graphic interviewing projectively to investigate modern Blood Indians' values about what was a good job for modern Bloods today. First Spindler used photographs as probes, but found that informants were so carried away with literal photographic information, that they never answered the key question, "What is a good job for modern Blood Indians?" So Spindler switched to occupational drawings, which gave the overview he needed (Spindler and Spindler, 1965). Goldschmidt also used drawings to projectively recover the circumstances of "the good life" for modern Menomini Indians (Goldschmidt and Edgerton, 1961).

Siegel of Stanford University studied Indian ceremonialism in Picuris, the smallest of the Rio Grande Pueblos. I made a community survey of Picuris culture and ecology to gather projective probes, which included photographs of an exquisite deer dance and records of ceremonial running on an ancient race track near the pueblo. This projective research revealed that running, rather than religious group dancing, was the center of ceremonialism. This threw new light on the ceremonial ethos of nearby Taos Pueblo, which shares the same language as Picuris.

The camera's technical ability for volume recording of information swiftly and accurately is a major contribution to research involving mass visual evidence. The camera's automative process and mechanical memory make it a rewarding tool in rapid reconnaissance, particularly of unfamiliar territory. The camera can record circumstances unfamiliar to the observer accurately, an opportunity that can speed up preliminary field work. As an example, in early research, we were able to survey village sites photographically that were wholly unfamiliar. In two hours of automobile cruising, we were able to photograph from the car window all the houses and town space of an extensive rural community. This housing file was later reviewed by a native consultant, who was able to give us all the inhabitants' names, locations, and activities.

In the Harvard Chiapas project George Collier and Evan Vogt carried this technique forward dramatically by using standard aerial photographs as keys to community mapping. The Chiapas project (Collier, 1974) found that Indian consultants could identify trails and community patterns responsibly from aerial records.

Community surveying goes beyond cartographic identity and includes the sociometric patterns of a community. In a summer's field project, it is possible to record all ceremonious and recreative gatherings and, with the aid of native consultants, identify all associations and community personalities. Of course, this approach has its hazards, and interviewing should be carried out ethically and in private, with trusted consultants.

Ekman, a psychologist, turned to mass recording by photography to study facial expressions. Ekman and Friesen (1974) of Langley Porter Institute stabilized expressions of the face by studying voluminous records of slides of the patients in the Langley Porter Clinic. Ekman assembled a visual "grammar" of facial signals to assist psychiatrists in recognizing the suppressed emotions so important in diagnosis. But Ekman's medical colleagues felt this index would be valid only in American society. Ekman suspected this was not the case, and tested the validity of universal facial signaling among the natives of New Guinea. He found that facial messages could be given and clearly received universally. Ekman warned that, as children matured, facial expressions became culturally directed, but if one knew the universal signaling, now and then the cultural curtain would part, and one could perceive the basic emotions within. This phenomenon was equally true at Langley Porter Clinic. Patients who were about to be released from the clinic could fool the doctors with diagnostically prescribed expressions of serenity. After release, some of these patients would commit suicide.

Another important function of photography is in recording cultural inventories. Again, the volume reportage possible with the camera is of essential importance. The cultural inventory can index a variety of research subjects, recording the content of native markets, inventorying who comes to the market, inventorying the content of habitations and the character and ownership of dwellings in a community. Roberts of Cornell University was the first innovator of the cultural inventory. In the 1950s, Roberts (1951) made a complete index of three Navajo Hogans in Ramah, New Mexico.

The cultural inventory has broad theoretical functions. The mass recording of the inventory, when structurally categorized into organized complexity, can reveal significant patterns that direct observation could miss.

For example, in 1952, we used the cultural inventory to find acculturation patterns in Navajo housing. I assisted Tremblay in making a survey of Navajo dwelling types in a Navajo agricultural community. This study was made on the Cornell Fruitland Project directed by Adair and Sasaki. The goal of the study was to find whether there was a relationship between dwelling types and general acculturation. In a few days, I was able to record the diversity of dwellings in this agricultural community. The sample moved from classical hogans, to tents, log cabins, stone houses, and homes built of variegated materials. We then related the dwellings to the project's personality file, which contained detailed information on the Fruitland Navajos. This supporting information revealed that there was a clear relation between habitations and acculturation (Tremblay, et al., 1954).

Associated with photographing the cultural inventory is also rapid photographic surveying—as an example, surveys of agricultural technology, plowing and harrowing carried out in ways that might create soil erosion, or evidence of contour cultivation that minimized erosion. With the camera a whole country's agricultural patterns could be recorded in a few days. Survey photography gathers evidence swiftly for detailed analysis later over weeks, months, and years.

Certainly, there are definite limitations to the still image. No matter how systematically exposures are made, the still records are time cuts that offer a static record. Still photography records artifacts, unchanging material that can be wholly studied in a single frame image, but a classroom is culture in motion, an unfolding drama through time. Further, the still image offers little psychological understanding—for still images do not qualify behavior, because psychological nuance is most clearly expressed in motion.

Hall had enriched his own nonverbal research with film. One 50-foot, Super-8 reel of film—two minutes of film—recorded how Pueblo Indians, Spanish Americans, and Anglo-Americans move through space. These observations, filmed at a fiesta in San Juan Pueblo, recorded how three ethnic families moved across the Plaza. When the film was screened at six frames a second, the families appeared as trained in their cultural routines as three companies of dancers. Similarly, at a medical conference in Palo Alto, Birdwhistell had analysed a two-minute film of a disturbed mother and child. He studied the film frame for frame and diagnosed the mother and child's problem as the "double bind." Psychiatrists attending this conference agreed that Birdwhistell's diagnosis was more accurate than one made by the family's doctor.

ANTHROPOLOGY'S RELUCTANCE TO USE NONVERBAL EVIDENCE

After thirty years of successful research with photography and visual anthropology, why has there not been a popular development in the use of nonverbal evidence? Visual anthropology has been clearly reviewed in many articles as well as in many widely circulated academic books. *Kinesics*, developed by Birdwhistell; *proxemics*, developed by Hall; and *choreometrics*, developed by Lomax, have become household words in cultural understanding, *but not the validity of the photographic record*. Basic field methods in anthropology move on much the same. Anthropologists make many transparencies that are screened in their classrooms as *illustrations*.

Ethnographic film increases in popularity and is granted ever larger endowments which escalate many film projects into epic productions. The technology grows increasingly complex, to the point where film is made only by trained professionals, a development that takes the camera not only out of the hands of the native, but out of reach of the field anthropologist as well. Film has become the popular image of anthropology, but film as a research undertaking rarely happens, even though Margaret Mead helped found the American Film Research Institute and The National Archives of Ethnographic Film in the Smithsonian Institution to promote cross-cultural research. We hear a lot about gathering *researchable film*, but the epic films are not made for their researchable ethnographic records, but for visual lectures in the teaching of anthropology.

Teaching anthropology with visual materials is an important development in visual anthropology. However, there is a great difference between using film primarily for illustration and using it to bring the field experience into the classroom. Students must make their own simulated first-hand observations and develop their own concepts about human development. Films that have been edited and structured to present an academic point of view, like all lectures, operate as a closed process and offer little inventive understanding. When a lecture film is screened, students internalize the *verbal* message and leave the room. But when an open-ended data film is shown, students are challenged to form their own concepts by researching the film record. This opportunity makes the study of culture alive, part of their own intelligence. Illustrative film has important function in presenting already established points of view, but they are after the fact and do not add to the record. Only the research process directly expands the cultural record.

Anthropology's support of epic film reflects the field's ambiguity over film for research. Few large-project research films are funded. There continue to be projects that incorporate still photography, but generally, in anthropology, still photographic records have been largely ignored as research data. Film as research is debated, and, regardless of the rise of epic ethnographic film, individual filmmakers like Timothy Asch, David MacDougall and John Marshall continue to make invaluable research film. Indeed, there is far more open ethnographic record film than there are funded projects in ethnographic film analysis.

The controversies over visual anthropology are not over reliable ethnographic film, but about film research itself. It is the information *in* the moving image that challenges the anthropological record, because film brings human behavior alive.

Film qualifies behavior, yielding information that is commonly missing from the verbal ethnographic record. As one example, the anthropological record of "primitive" peoples, by default, too often omit observations on the human nature and refinements of materially underdeveloped people. Films of the Kalihari by Marshall reveal that these hunters were sensitive and intelligent people, regardless of their low material state.

Film is an artifact that reflects much of the subtlety that anthropologists discipline out of their writing; hence, photography could expand the tangibility of the anthropological record. Film reflects the "software" that scientific record, by default, omits. The methods of film research are more holistic than the disciplines of classical research. Hall suggests that the realistic complexity of film requires all sensory intellectual reactions to be spontaneously awake, as in our response to real circumstance. Hall cautions his students about the stricture resulting from first analysing film with a "closed process." Hall believes the researcher should first allow the film data to "affect" the research in order to develop a structured approach that retains the authenticity of film as primary experience. Researching film also requires whole reason, including the intuitive spatial understandings of the right hemisphere of intelligence, followed by the disciplined analysis promoted by the left hemisphere. Filmic insights may also suggest an implicit criticism of the scope of anthropology. I believe both the research philosophy of film analysis and breadth of its revelations have created a criticism of the film record.

At the 1979 meetings of the American Anthropological Association, there were many papers on the reflexivity of the anthropological record, and, in particular, the reflexivity of film. The overkill of this self-concern suggested that you cannot safely research film until you check out the bias and emotionality of the filmmaker. This reaction may be realistically directed to the epic anthropological film that tends to reflect the belief system of the producer-editor. Yet film exposed as data does not contain this distortion of reflexivity, for the important experiments in film research are carried out on footage of only two minutes. I asked a professor who participated in this reflexivity symposium,

> What if you applied your criteria of non-reflexivity to the general field of anthropological literature, how much would remain responsible?

His answer:

> None.

A strong case is the writings of Oscar Lewis and of Robert Redfield who both studied the Mexican community, Tepotzlan, and wrote wholly contradictory texts. Redfield, when challenged by students, made this statement:

I believe the "good life" takes place in small organizations and my research in anthropology has been to demonstrate this. . . . Now Oscar Lewis is from New York City and cannot stand small organizations, so he has written about all the disturbing realities of living in a little community. . . . His observations are correct. . . . Read both books! (Personal Communication)

Indeed, anthropology is one of the most reflexive fields of the behavioral sciences. Much information is gained through intense person-to-person communication and there is necessarily much uncontrollable field research. This open nature of investigation questions the scientific nature of anthropology.

Reflexivity is an important insight of visual anthropology and the essence of information gathered in interviewing with photographic probes. Reflexivity in this circumstance unlocks value sentiments and the memory of the consultant which are otherwise unrevealed. A very important experiment in programmed reflexivity was Sol Worth and John Adair's experiment (1972) *Through Navajo Eyes* Worth and Adair taught 16 mm filmmaking to a Navajo team of three women and three men. They mastered the Bell and Howell three turret lens camera and Weston light meter in three days, and in five weeks, each photographer made two films. They projected on film how Navajos perceive their world and relate their lives to its ecology. The narrative pattern of these records also revealed the circular process of their communications, which correlated with Navajo linguistics and mythology. When film is made objectively to gather information and responsible evidence, it can be the most non-reflexive and "clean" data in anthropology. The disciplined film record can allow the ethnographer to describe, without personal projection, refinements of behavior and environment otherwise scientifically impossible to define.

The validity of the film record was the subject of a conversation between Margaret Mead and Gregory Bateson in 1976—a significant communication in the evolution of visual anthropology ("For God's Sake, Margaret," 1976). Mead and Bateson are the symbolic and real parents of photography in anthropology. Discussing the scientific integrity of film evidence at a 1979 symposium on reflexivity in film and anthropology, Mead suggested that the only way to control reflexivity in film was to lock the camera position, turn on the shutter and film transport, and leave the room. Bateson rejected this process and pointed out that you must move around to record behavior wholly. This conflict of reason between these innovators' photographic research suggests the conflict over visual anthropology; the exploration of technology on one hand, and the refinement of human instrumentalization on the other. Could we get scientifically rewarding interviews by turning on the recorder and leaving the room?

The accepted use of photography in the hard sciences suggests the conflicts over visual anthropology are deeper than this technical conversation between Mead and Bateson. First, anthropology is a highly verbal field and is getting more so every year as the literary feedback increases in volume. The training of anthropologists is primarily in knowing the literature.

Historically, anthropology has been a scholarly pursuit with an established European background going back to Frazer and *The Golden Bough*. Its European tradition is elite, founded in intellectualism. The nonverbal was lower caste communication. Words, literate and spoken, are as essential to the anthropologist as the telescope is to the astronomer. Words magnify truth and validate authenticity. The research process itself is one of converting information into a verbal code that transfers significance into cognition and literature. The intensity of this verbal effort tempts the ethnographer to become a computer programmer, not a firsthand observing field worker. Hence, both background and style of anthropology reasonably alienate anthropologists from nonverbal responses.

I do not suggest that social science can pliantly shift from the intellectual to the sensual, regardless of the importance of the visual, for the verbal computing process is essential to research, as analytic cognition. But anthropology needs a recording technology to gather visual information objectively, swiftly, and accurately. Photography could be an intelligence bridge between sensual contextural reason and intellectual analysis.

These observations attempt to define the block between anthropology and visual, sensual communication. Visual responses are interpreted as "feeling" as compared to "thinking." Cognitively, the block may be further complicated by the intangibility of visual, sensual communication. When the consultant speaks, the anthropologist is the receptor of the message. When the communication is visual and sensual, reception can become blurred by the receptivity of the observer. Only if the consultant tells the interviewer about his or her world image can the message be coded into reason. If the consultant is nonverbal, there is no way the anthropologist can share world vision. There must be a visual artifact that can be studied rationally before we can share one's vision of the world.

I teach both art students who have divorced themselves from verbal and linear cognition and anthropology students who have lost touch with sensuality and never found the nonlinear world of organic creativity. I am working with prisoners of two extremes of intelligence; the worlds of "software" and "hardware." The holistic record of film and photography could function to bring these extremes into one whole intelligence.

REFERENCES

COLLIER, G. (1974). The impact of airphoto-technology on the study of demography and ecology in Highland Chiapas. *In* E.Z. Vogt (Ed.), "Aerial Photography in Anthropological Field Research." Cambridge, MA: Harvard University Press.

COLLIER, J., Jr. (1957). Photography in anthropology: A report on two experiments. *American Anthropologist 59,* 843-859.

EKMAN, P., and FRIESEN, W.V. (1974). "Unmasking the Face." Englewood Cliffs, NJ: Prentice-Hall.

"For God's Sake, Margaret!" Conversation with Gregory Bateson and Margaret Mead. (1976). *Coevolution Quarterly* (Summer).

GOLDSCHMIDT, W., and EDGERTON, R.B. (1961). A picture technique for the study of values. *American Anthropologist 63,* 26-47.

ROBERTS, J.M. (1951). Three Navajo households: A comparative study of small group culture. *Papers of the Peabody Museum of American Archeology and Ethnology 40* (No. 3).

SPINDLER, G., and SPINDLER, L. (1965). The instrumental activities inventory: A technique for the study of the psychology of acculturation. *Southwestern Journal of Anthropology 21,* 1-23.

TREMBLAY, M.A., COLLIER J., Jr., and SASAKI, T.T. (1954). Navajo housing in transition. *America Indigena 14,* 187-218.

WORTH, S., and ADAIR, J. (1972). "Through Navajo Eyes: An Exploration in Film Communication and Anthropology." Indianapolis, IN: Indiana University Press.

18

The Theory and Practice of Content Analysis in Marxist Communication Science

HOWARD H. FREDERICK, JR.
Ohio University
Athens, Ohio 45701

Analysis of communication content can provide both descriptive and predictive data on human behavior. Yet Marxist communication scholars have warned that content analysis as practiced in the West is a class-bound, ahistorical technique based on false theoretical and philosophical premises. They assert that the technique does have merit, however, when certain methodological considerations are taken into account. This paper scrutinizes content analysis in the light of Marxist social thought. It first reviews the underpinnings of content analysis as elaborated in the West and in Eastern Europe. It then reviews several content analysis studies that have appeared in Poland, Democratic Germany, and elsewhere to see if theory fits practice. It concludes with a discussion of how to strengthen this social science research technique wherever it finds application.*

CONTENT ANALYSIS: THE CLASSICAL DEFINITION

Perhaps the most widely accepted definition of content analysis was formulated by Bernard Berelson (1952, p. 18):

*The author wishes to thank Dr. Walery Pisarek and Dr. Zbigniew Sobiecki of the Press Research Centre, Krakow, Poland, for their encouragement and comments on an earlier draft. The author is also grateful to Dr. Wolfgang Kleinwächter, Institute for International Studies, Karl Marx University, Leipzig, GDR, for assistance in locating materials. The paper's strengths are due in part to these three scholars; the failings, however, are the author's sole responsibility.

Content analysis is the research technique for the objective, systematic, and quantitative description of the manifest content of communication.

Berelson insisted on *objectivity;* each step must be so formulated that no error or bias creeps into the design that might reflect the subjective predisposition of the researcher. He stipulates that the description be *quantitative;* if the attribute cannot be counted, it is not present. Finally, he restricts analysis only to *manifest* content of the message, i.e., to attributes that lie "on the surface."

THE STUDY OF CONTENT ANALYSIS IN EASTERN EUROPE

Though content analysis has been used in the West for over 80 years, socialist communication science only in the 1970s began to formulate a theory and practice of content analysis. Because of a virulent state-supported anti-intellectualism during the Stalin era and the bourgeois background of many university faculty, all social science experienced unprecedented repression. Sociology and social psychology, from which content analysis sprang in the West, were "for Marxism superfluous." Such methods as opinion polls, surveys, and content analysis were forbidden, since, it was argued, "in socialism opinion is not researched, it is formed" (Karbusicky, 1970).

Only Kruschchev's denunciation of Stalinist orthodoxy began to relieve the pressure. By 1964 there was a change. A conference of social scientists organized by the Academy of Sciences of the USSR called for the "old-fashioned dogmatism of Stalinist days to be replaced by a more flexible policy in which at least a limited objectivity would be permissible." (Simerenko, 1969, p. 15).

By 1969, fully three decades after its elaboration in the West, content analysis found its place amid the pages of the prestigious *Voprosy Filosofii* (Problems of Philosophy) (Korobeinikov, 1969). Today concentrated efforts are underway to create a theory of content analysis based on a scientific worldview and Marxist-Leninist methodology. For example, a collective of authors from the Journalism Department of the Karl Marx University in Leipzig (1977) prepared its first major work on the purpose and function of content analysis. (A summary of this report is in Skaun and Tiedke, 1977.)

THE MARXIST CRITIQUE OF CONTENT ANALYSIS

Marxist social scientists believe that content analysis is based on false theoretical premises. It exists in an ahistorical vacuum disconnected from the very society it attempts to analyze. It does not make the societal macro-connections. It concentrates on being correct in technical methods at the expense of being loose on the conceptual level. To the Marxist social scientist, there is no such thing as objective truth that is perceivable by an unbiased social scientist. All research is rooted in the fundamental ideology of the scientist and his discipline. Ideology, one's overall conception of the world, one's belief system, derives from the interests of the social class to which one belongs. Such class interests are the result of the material conditions that prevail in that society.

Marxism believes that truth is historically conditioned, that class-bound ideology is inevitable. As Lenin (1972, p. 135) said, "Historically conditioned are the circumstances under which we make progress in our knowledge of the essence of things." The task, he said, is to create a "scientific ideology," one that adheres to the fundamental science of dialectical change in society. Though absolute truth is as yet unknown, and since ideology is unavoidable, adopting a scientific ideology will add new fragments of truth to human knowledge. "Human thought then by its nature is capable of giving, and does give, absolute truth, which is composed of the sum-total of relative truths" (Lenin, 1927, p. 133).

In a theoretical sense, then, content analysis cannot be truly scientific unless it serves consciously a scientific ideology. Otherwise it becomes an "end-in-itself," disconnected from reality. Content analysis must be used instrumentally, i.e., in relation to the societal context. To the Marxist, the technique becomes concrete only to the extent that it fulfills its ideological obligation to criticize capitalist society.

In addition, Marxists believe that content analysis rests on a false philosophical premise—Freudian-based depth psychology, particularly in relation to sign formation. A sign is a word or "signal" that stands for something in experience. The word "house" stands for a generalized experience that humans have with four-walled, roofed structures. In Western linguistic psychology, the sign is really shorthand for a unique concept of a house that *resides in the mind.* It exists separately from the material world, and its meaning resides in the world of ideas.

But to the dialectical materialist, this is reversed. Signs (and all cognitive processes, for that matter) are not ideas within the mind but direct manifestations of the material world. Everything that exists—language, religion, psychology, emotion, even knowledge—comes into being as a result of material causes, not mental processes. To the Marxist, individual cognition and sign formation are social facts. They are reflections, copies, photographs, mirror-reflections of real things and processes of nature (Lenin, 1927, p. 237ff). Signs are not created by the mind but "are conditioned above all by social organization of the participants involved and also by the immediate conditions of their interaction" (Voloshinov, 1973, p. 21).

Signs in themselves are neutral; the same language can be used by peoples of opposing ideologies. But signs are the "base" that forms the social lens through which ideological meaning is refracted. The base supports the "superstructure," which refers to "legal, political, religious, aesthetic, or philosophic—in short, ideological—form" (Mandel, 1969, p. 45).

Thus content analysis of words (signs) in the Marxist purview should be used not to infer psychic processes but to infer social, "superstructural" phenomena. For example, the tendency in the West to use content analysis to analyze cognitive processes of individual decision-makers is subjectivist and idealist. It does not examine the ideological structure of the society that motivates individual actors.

From these theoretical and philosophical considerations, applicable to all or "bourgeois" social science, we now move to particular Marxist criticism of content analysis as a method. We can examine these objections by recalling Berelson's definition quoted above: "the objective, systematic, and quantitative description of the manifest content of communication."

To begin, there is no such thing as objectivity even in Marxism. All perception is class-bound. Try as he or she might, a scientist ultimately cannot escape the limitations of acculturation, social and physical environment, historical and ideological circumstances. This is in direct contradiction to the fundamental axiom of Western social science that opens objective investigation to all who abide by its canons, without regard to the class, status or power of the investigator.

But what do bourgeois social scientists mean by objectivity? In general, they mean shutting out the researcher's subjective influences on data gathering and analysis, and thereby on the results of the study. Of course, one should not denigrate this effort, for it is a necessary precondition for objectivity. But, as Skaun and Tiedke emphasize, "to meet this crucial criterion of objectivity requires the availability of a scientifically proven, ideologically theoretical and methodological basis for applied social research, for only such a basis makes it possible to have an objective view of society and of the journalistic products that result from the society."

Bourgeois social science cannot meet this task because of its continued adherence to neo-positivism and pure empiricism, which disregard existing social macro-relations and which do not automatically lend themselves to a critique of domination. Content analysis in the West, with rare exceptions,[1] has refused to deal with the predominant macrorelation of communication— the social determinism of the bourgeois press by the monopoly capital system of domination. Bourgeois content analysis has analyzed social phenomena

---

[1]Two studies by Gerbner (1961, 1964), early in his career, investigated the question of ideology in news. Dovring (1975) examined the ideological and political setting in which communication takes place. Arora and Lasswell (1969) did an extensive survey of the role of ideology in the elite press of India and the United States.

eclectically, often describing them without drawing the far-reaching theoretical implications.

Empirical fact dominates in Western content analysis to the point where it becomes a fetish. As Mattelart (1973, p. 28) has pointed out, capitalism creates fetishes to fortify its rationale of social domination:

> To create a fetish or to elevate a process or phenomenon to the level of a fetish means "to crystalize it in the form of an object set apart," to remove it from the actual conditions of its production.

By fetishizing fact, bourgeois content analysis fails to connect fact with theory. It cannot reach the roots of socio-economic phenomena and relations. It is blind to the essence of social processes.

This should come as no surprise, since content analysis had its very birth within the political economy of capitalism. Barcus (1959) surveyed over 1700 content analysis studies going back to the 1890s. He chronicled how the method served the expanding market for readers at the turn of the century.

Content analysis, like other Western communication science methodologies, followed the exigencies of the commercial market place and the world political scene. Survey research quickly developed in sophistication because of the availability of commercial funds (Tunstall 1977, p. 204). Audience effects research, demographic profiles, public policy analysis, communication, and development—all, in Schiller's words (1976, p. 19). "parall[ed] and undergird[ed] the corporate system that financed most of it." Content analysis was no exception.

Further detracting from the objectivity of content analysis is the Marxist view of the class nature of language. The chief fault of the positivist and idealist approach to language that characterizes Western content analysis is that "it separates thought from language and language from the history of people" (Schmalstieg, 1969, p. 361). Language and ideology are inextricably connected. A critical reader of international news knows within a few sentences what class interest or ideology is being represented. "The deposed ruler" and "the overthrown tyrant" may describe the same person, but they employ different attitudes toward his demise. "Language does not lie; on the contrary, it is the truth of the ideology it expresses" (Calvet, 1972, p. 15).

This critique then belies Berelson's insistence on objectivity. But it also confronts another mandate of Berelson's definition—that content analysis must limit itself to analyzing the manifest content (the surface meaning) of the message. To Berelson, it is inappropriate to use the technique to analyze deeper meanings, namely the relationship of signs to those who produce or receive them. But the Marxist believes that it is precisely in the latent structure of meaning (and in the sign-source and the sign-recipient relationship) where the ideological dimensions of content lie. By not studying the hidden levels, the message becomes a shadow of the original reality, totally denuded of its richness and ideological connotations.

Were it not restricted to manifest content, the technique would still be hampered by the third proscription of Berelson, that it can be quantitative. To be fair, this proscription has received its share of criticism from Western social scientists who believe that such quantitative limitations lead to a bias in selecting problems to be investigated and to undue emphasis on precision at the cost of significance. As Halloran (1974, p. 12) has said, "How valuable is it to be precise and consistent about something that isn't true or doesn't matter?"

Such "hyperscientific" empiricism considers each case in isolation. The laws of Marxist dialectics, on the other hand, refuse to think of things each by itself. Marxism recognizes that all material things emerge, live, and die in an unending process of change, each thing connected immutably to, and continually changed by, every other thing. So it is with quantity and quality.

All change has a quantitative aspect in which a mere increase or decrease of an attribute does not alter the essential quality of the object. For example, as water is heated from 0 to 100 degrees Centigrade, depending on atmospheric pressure, it remains a fluid. But such quantitative change cannot go on forever. At a certain point—what Hegel called the nodal point—there must be a qualitative change. In this case, the liquid becomes a gas.

Qualitative change is always the sum of quantitative changes. Differences in quality are based on difference in quantity. In content analysis, the quantitative is the basic measure, but it must be employed as a yardstick to qualitative measurement. For example, a simple frequency measure of a particular attribute in the message cannot exist in isolation but must lead to qualitative interpretation about the environment of the source.

HOW MARXIST COMMUNICATIONS SCHOLARS USE CONTENT ANALYSIS

Despite the many Marxist criticisms of the philosophical, theoretical, and technical faults of content analysis, there has been a general willingness among Eastern European communication researchers to adapt and develop the technique. Korobeinikov (1969) asserted that the methods of content analysis could play an important role in the understanding of social processes. He believed that the study of these methods of content analysis could play an important role in the understanding of social processes. He believed that the study of these methods of content analysis could play an important role in the understanding of social processes. He believed that the study of these methods could enrich Soviet sociology." Since his article appeared in 1969, numerous content analysis studies have appeared in scholarly socialist communication journals throughout Eastern Europe.

To see how Marxist communication researchers have used these theories in their applied research, I turned to 32 content analysis studies which appeared in communications publications in Eastern Europe during the period 1973-1978. These studies were abstracted by CECOM: Central European Mass Communication Research Documentation Centre in Krakow, Poland. Countries represented in this sample were Poland, Yugoslavia, Bulgaria, Czechoslovakia, the Soviet Union, and the German Democratic Republic.[2]

It is quickly apparent that content analysis is used for instrumental purposes in advising editors and media decision-makers. Drastich's (1973) results were "helpful to the editorial board" of the Slovak *Sport* magazine in promoting athletic education. Kubiak et al. (1974) analyzed letters to the editor of the *Krakow Gazette* to describe their writers' motivations, social tensions apparent in the letters, and the newspaper's response. Brandt (1975) analyzed editorials in seven Democratic German dailies to see if their subjects were consistent with Party directives. Splichal (1976) analyzed over 9,000 messages received by Radio-Television Ljubljana to determine which types of messages were then retransmitted by these media. Zachejova (1975) scrutinized selected Slovak illustrated weeklies to see to what extent the content diverged from editorial policies.

There was also a great concern among the content analysis studies in this sample for the socialization processes, i.e., education for socialism. Maliszewski and Rusinek (1973) looked at hero roles presented in the Polish youth press to ascertain how modern socialist values were being disseminated, while Stojak (1975) did the same on Serbo-Croatian comic books. Splichal (1974) reviewed Yugoslav TV "interpretive news" to find out which content characteristics produced positive and which produced negative attitudes toward Yugoslav politics. Maslyk (1974) considered how the factory newspaper of the Warsaw metal works was satisfying the information needs of its workers.

Several studies used content analysis in a comparative fashion to describe the differing ideological content of foreign and domestic news. Myslinski (1973) delved back into Polish history to describe the difference in coverage of turn-of-the-century socialist and conservative newspapers. Dubiel (1975) analyzed book reviews that appeared in *Journalism Quarterly* (US), *Publizistik* (FRG), and *Zeszyty Prasoznawcze* (Poland) to determine whether those communication journals were open to alternative ideological viewpoints. Lewartowska (1978) described the coverage of Poland in *Le Monde, Frankfurter Allgemeine Zeitung,* and the *International Herald Tribune* and of

---

[2]*CECOM: Central European Mass Communication Research Documentation Centre* is published in English by the Press Research Centre, Uynek Glowny 23, 31-008 Krakow, Poland. Approximately 200 articles are abstracted each year.

France, the Federal Republic of Germany, and the United States in *Trybuna Ludu*.

The categories used in these studies are frequently the same as those used in the West: geographical region covered; subject classifications such as the economy of defense. The units of measurement also are similar: words, themes, frequency, etc. But there is no hesitation to use "value-laden" categories such as sensationalist, capitalist, or enemies of the state. Inferences based on content characteristics can range deeply into the mind of the sender or into the motivations of the receiver.

STRENGTHENING CONTENT ANALYSIS THROUGH MARXIST SOCIAL THOUGHT

The following suggestions might strengthen the use of content analysis in the West.

First, many non-Marxist theorists have said that quantitative and qualitative research are not dichotomous attributes but fall along a continuum, that both methods are useful and should be seen as complementary, and that insights are to be gained when a researcher moves back and forth between these approaches. Additionally, attention should be paid to those processes that accumulate in quantity only to undergo a permanent qualitative change. Such a change leaves behind one continuum and engages another.

Second, to avoid the criticism that content analysis is an end-in-itself, disconnected from reality, the researcher should endeavor to contrast and correlate content findings with non-content indices of the same variable. In a study of newspaper coverage of the oil crisis, for example, content data might be contrasted with trade figures, petroleum consumption, and import-export data that also might indicate relative preoccupation with oil. Content data must continually be put into proportion, either as percentages of appearance relative to other attributes in the same text, or in the context of non-content data. In the same way, the whole research design must be seen in its societal and historical context.

Third, further thought must be given to the relevance of units of analysis (word, item, paragraph, statement) in the light of Marxist theory. The researcher's choice of such units doubtless is one of the most ideologically pregnant moments of the research process. In the Soviet Union, for example, one measuring unit is the "judgment" (Russian: suschdenie). This is, I believe, close to what Osgood et al. (1956) have called the "evaluative assertion," or what Gerbner (1964) has called the "proposition." In this way we can combine the normative expression of ideology with the empirical rigor of measurement.

Next, researchers must cast their research in a comparative design that analyzes documents of conflicting ideologies (as determined by non-content indices). For example, Frederick (1981) has applied various content measures to newscasts of the Voice of America and Radio Havana Cuba in an attempt to evaluate the effectiveness of these measures in determining ideology.

Finally, and most importantly, I would argue for a value-directed rather than a value-free research attitude. Social research is not conducted in an antiseptic laboratory. It is conducted in the real world, whose impact on us is inescapable. The very selection of the research problem is conditioned in part by our historical and societal circumstances. Rather than ignoring this, we must relish it. But to be fair to our colleagues and our craft, our value direction must be explicit and without apology, so that the criticism may be directed as much to the values as to the theory and the methodology. We must not shirk the "marketplace of ideas," for there is a resounding similarity between the Marxist concept that "absolute truth is the sum of relative truths" and the libertarian, self-righting process in which the truth will out among all the disparate voices.

REFERENCES

ARORA, S.K., and LASSWELL, H.D. (1969). "Political Communication: The Public Language of Elites in India and the United States." New York: Holt, Rinehart and Winston.

BARCUS, F.E. (1959). "Communications Content: Analysis of the Research, 1900-1958." Unpublished dissertation, University of Illinois.

BERELSON, B. (1952). "Content Analysis in Communication Research." Glencoe, IL: Free Press.

BRANDT, K. (1975). The function and formation of "Editorial Leaders" in the daily press. *Theorie und Praxis des sozialistischen Journalismus* (Leipzig) *1*, 47-52. (In German.)

CALVET, L.J. (1972). Langage de classe: Lutte de classe. *Politique Hebdo* (27 Jan.) 15.

DOVRING, K. (1975). "Frontiers of Communications: The Americas in Search of Political Culture." Boston, MA: Christopher House.

DRASTICH, O. (1973). Attempt at a quantitative content analysis of the daily journal. *"Sport." Otazky Zurnalistiky 16*, 32-38. (In Slovakian.)

DUBIEL, P. (1975). Comparative analysis of the book reviews in three press research periodicals: *Journalism Quarterly, Publizistik, Zeszyty Prasoznawcze. Zeszyty Prasznawcze 17* (No. 1), 27-44. (In Polish.)

FREDERICK, H.H. (1981). Ideology in international newscasting: Radio warfare between the Voice of American and Radio Havana Cuba. *Potomac Review* (Spring), 1 ff.

GERBNER, G. (1961). Press perspective in world communications: A pilot study, *Journalism Quarterly 38*, 313-322.

GERBNER, G. (1964). Ideological perspectives and political tendencies in news reporting. *Journalism Quarterly 41*, 495-509.

HALLORAN, J.D. (1974). "Mass Media and Society: The Challenge of Research." Leicester, England: Leicester University Press.

KARBUSICKY, V. (1970). Inhaltsanalyse in Rahmen der Ideologie. *Publizistic (Konstanz) 15*, 344.

Karl Marx University. Journalism Department. (1977). "Forschungsbericht: Zur Methodik der Inhaltsanalyse Journalisticher Produkte." Leipzig: Sektion Journalistik, Karl Marx University.

KOROBEINIKOV, V.W. (1969). Analis soderzhaniua v massovoy dommunikatii. (Content analysis of mass communication). *Voprosy Filosofii* (Moscow) *27*, 100-110.

KUBIAK, H., FILAS, R., GERULA, M., KRUPSKA, H., MOS, M., and ZIELINSKI, A. (1974). "The Expectations and Aspirations of Residents of the Cracow Region in the Light of Letters to the Editor of 'Gazeta Krakowska.' " Krakow: Instytut Sociologii Uniwersytetu Jagiellon-skiego. (In Polish.)

LENIN, V.I. (1927). "Materialism and Empiro-Criticism: Critical Comments on a Reactionary Philosophy." New York: International Publishers.

LEWARTOWSKA, Z. (1978). Images of countries presented in the press and the reality: Poland as presented in *Le Monde, Frankfurter Allgemeine Zeitung,* and *International Herald Tribune*—France, FRG, and USA as presented in *Trybuna Ludu. Zeszyty Prasoznawcze 19,* 25-44. (In Polish.)

MALISZEWSKI, A., and RUSINEK, A. (1973). Educative contents of the youth press. *In* "Tresci wychowawcze w prasie a poglady i postawy mlodziezy-Osrodek Badan Prasoznawczych RSW 'Prass.' " pp. 5-57. Krakow. (In Polish.)

MANDEL, W.M. (1969). Soviet Marxism and social science. *In* A. Simerenko (Ed.), "Social Thought in the Soviet Union." Chicago, IL: Quadrangle Books.

MASLYK, E. (1974). The plant press and the demand for information. *Zeszyty Prasoznawcze 15* (No. 3), 37-48. (In Polish.)

MATTELART, A. (1973). "La Comunicacion Masiva en el Proceso de Liberacion." Mexico, DF: Siglo Veintiuno Editores.

MYSLINSKI, J. (1973). Studies of the layout of the contents of the Polish daily press at the turn of the century: The conservative and socialist press. *Rocznik Historii Czasopismiennictwa Poliskiego 12,* 187-210. (In Polish.)

OSGOOD, C.E., SAPORTA, S., and NUNNALLY, J.C. (1956). Evaluative assertion analysis. *Litera* (Istanbul) *3,* 47-102.

SCHILLER, H.I. (1976). "Communication and Cultural Domination." White Plains, NY: International Arts and Sciences Press.

SCHMALSTIEG, W.R. (1969). Structural linguistics in the Soviet Union. *In* A. Simirenko (Ed.), "Social Thought in the Soviet Union." Chicago, IL: Quadrangle Books.

SIMERENKO, A. (1969). The development of Soviet social science. *In* A. Simerenko (Ed.), "Social Thought in the Soviet Union." Chicago, IL: Quadrangle Books.

SKAUN, W., and TIEDKE, W. (1977). Methodische Erfordernisse bei der Durchführung von Inhaltsanalysen journalisticher Produkte. *Theorie und Praxis des Sozialistischen Journalismus 4,* 43-51.

SKAUN, W., and TIEDKE, W. (1978). Was ist, was soll, was kann die Inhaltsanalyse? Überlegungen zur Bestimmung ihrer Wesensmerkmale und Anwendungsmöglichkeiten. *Theorie und Praxis des Sozialistischen Journalismus 1,* 42-50.

SPLICHAL, S. (1974). "Socializing Contents on the Television." Ljubljana: Sluzba za studij program RTV Ljubljana. (In Slovenian.)

SPLICHAL, S. (1976). "Information flow in Radio and Television." Ljubljana: Sluzba za studij programa RTV Ljubljana. (In Slovenian.)

STOJAK, R. (1975). The structure of comics. *Pregled 65,* 459-472. (In Serbo-Croatian.)

TUNSTALL, J. (1977). "The Media Are American: Anglo-American Media in the World." New York: Columbia University Press.

VOLOSHINOV, V.N. (1973). "Marxism and the Philosophy of Language." New York: Seminar Press.

ZACHEJOVA, V. (1975). "Slovak Illustrated Weeklies in the Light of Content Analysis: Experimental Research." Bratislava, CSSR: Institut pre vyskum masovych komunikacnuch prostriedkov. (In Slovak.)

PART **V**

COMMUNICATION
AND EDUCATION

19

Concepts and Uncertainty

ROBERT E. PROBST
Georgia State University
Atlanta, Georgia 30303

A child needs to know the difference between a sidewalk and a highway—
that's a concept necessary for survival. On the other hand, a child whose
notion of transportation is tightly bound to sidewalks and highways will never
invent the airplane. Schools need to train children both to stay out of the
way of trucks and to invent airplanes. That is to say, they have an obligation
to teach the concepts necessary for survival and to cultivate a tentativeness
toward established concepts that will enable a child to revise or replace them.
Perhaps the schools also have a third obligation—to look closely at what they
are teaching, in an effort to discover those concepts that are being communicated inadvertently, simply because they have become such a part of
what we casually call "reality" that we fail to see them, fail to recognize that
they are not the actual concrete substance of our experience, but rather,
organizing principles by which we impose some comprehensible order on
that experience.

The schools typically have discharged the first of these obligations fairly
well. They, with the help of parents, television, and whoever or whatever
else participates in the education of the child, have generally been able to
transmit the established concepts of the culture. They have not, however,
done quite as well in developing a willingness to reconsider the established
concepts and to search for and examine those entrenched concepts that have
come to be accepted as physical reality itself. Insofar as the schools fail to
encourage students to look curiously and skeptically at their own reality,
they allow students to remain trapped within a particular vision of the world.

When the schools present a particular vision of reality—that is to say,
a particular set of concepts—as though it were reality itself, then they pre-
dispose children to accept ideologies uncritically. They fail to teach children
that concepts are not permanent, unchanging attributes of the physical world,

but rather are human creations—imperfect, malleable representations of experience. Children who come to believe rigidly in the permanence and immutability of concepts are trapped by them, constrained by narrow, unchanging visions of love, justice, virtue, happiness, and the other important concepts around which we organize our lives. The absolute, unchanging nature of those visions confines the student, encouraging him or her to reject or ignore new information that might not be consistent with the vision he or she holds. Students trained to be absolutists, to believe in the permanence of conceptions, and to believe that knowledge is something given them by someone else, are prepared only for discipleship.

A discussion of "romantic love," might serve as an example of one of those concepts so pervasive in our culture that it works its effects almost unobserved. Romantic love seems to be one of those concepts that has come to be accepted as reality itself.

High school students questioned about their notions of love have left me with the impression that most of them view love as something into which they "fall." It is something over which they have no control. Few of them speak of love in terms of choosing, creating, building, sustaining—love may find them, or they may stumble into it, but it is not something that submits to the control of the intellect. The concept of love that seems to be most widely held is that it is a force operating independently in the world.

The suggestion that love might be something else is unlikely to find a warm reception. Several students, to whom I suggested that life would be much simpler and happier if we resolved to love a mate chosen for us by an expert trained to arrange marriages, responded that the idea was disgusting, that it would never work. When I suggested that someone trained to do the job might create the ideal relationship, they claimed that such a relationship would be unnatural, that love was something you fell into, not something you built or molded. All in all, my suggestion was found repugnant, stupid, and so alien to most of the students that it was inconceivable.

I wasn't surprised that the notion disgusted them—I shared the feeling. A member of the same culture, I hold many of the same feelings and opinions. But I was bothered by the rigidity of their notion. They were at least unwilling, and probably unable, to conceive of an alternate view of the relationship between men and women. The idea of the marriage broker was inconceivable for them, despite the fact that it was not only conceivable, but also practiced, in other cultures, even in contemporary cultures. Their concept of love and marriage was so firmly entrenched that it had become a part of the real, physical world for them. It was not a conceptual tool, but reality itself.

The point is not that romantic love is an inadequate concept, but rather, that it is such a firmly entrenched and unquestioned concept. The students were not in the least tentative about it. Their certainty prevents them from modifying their concepts of love in response to new experiences, new ideas, new information. Unless they come to recognize that it is a malleable formulation and not an immutable fact of life, they are likely to try continuously to force their experiences to fit the patterns of the concept they hold, rather than adjust the concept to fit the experiences they encounter.

There are, of course, innumerable notions that are similarly prone to reification. Thus, one of the principle obligations of the schools, if they are to encourage intellectual progress, is to cultivate tentativeness about the concepts by which we run our lives, to make explicit the notion that concepts are created and recreated, that they are not simply floating free in the natural world, waiting to be discovered, and to thus encourage in students a cautious and questioning attitude. Students must be invited to participate in shaping and reshaping their conceptions, feeding their thought with reading and discussion that demonstrate various perspectives, different attitudes and ideas.

Such a concept as "power" is, then, not that offered by the dictionary. Rather it is the notion built from discussing *Macbeth, All the King's Men,* the distribution of authority within the school, political events. Teaching students to form concepts on the basis of experience (including that of reading, of course), and to re-form them on the basis of further experience, may cultivate in them the tolerance for uncertainty and ambiguity necessary to avoid imprisonment by visions of the world grown solid and unbending.

Students may be invited to practice the reshaping of concepts if works are appropriately grouped and questions appropriately raised to force students to draw distinctions between the visions presented in different works. Our literature, however—both the written word and film and television—tends largely to sustain some of those concepts that might profitably be questioned. In the absence of differing notions and other concepts, dominant myths all difficult to examine. We may encounter variations on the theme, but we are unlikely to find radically different tunes.

Still, even when patterns are so deeply engrained in the culture, close attention to the values and the assumptions represented in the text may reveal them. The challenge is to speed the evolution of ideas by looking for those ideas that have become so deeply embedded in our thoughts that we are unaware of them. Clearly, finding those concepts is not something that can be done methodically and regularly—like any hunt, it requires a great deal of attention and luck. The society has, however, demonstrated that it is capable of ferreting out the hidden assumption and transforming it. The attack on racism, and the more recent attack on sexism, are examples of this process.

It may, of course, be over-optimistic to assume that discovering, revealing, and discussing the concepts that make up reality for this culture will be sufficient to enable people to modify those concepts and their behavior. But it seems, nonetheless, that those discoveries and discussions would be a necessary first step toward change.

20

Teaching Communication Competence in the Native American Studies Program*

WILLIAM R. KENNAN
West Texas State University
Canyon, Texas 79016

PHILIP D. LUJAN
University of Oklahoma
Norman, Oklahoma 73019

DAVID H. DOBKINS
University of Southwest Louisiana
Lafayette, Louisiana 70504

The classroom behavior of Native American college students has long stimulated the curiosity and frustration of teachers and researchers. These behavioral patterns are complex and their origins and purposes difficult to identify, making effective teaching and counseling difficult. Several explanations exist, but they are often cultural presumptions with regard to the nature of educational institutions and/or the cultures involved. In addition, very little of such explanatory research offers practical guidance to the teacher.

The purpose of this paper is not to reanalyze or add to the already formidable body of literature on the subject. Rather, its purpose is to draw out of the literature a tentative explanation and description of Native American classroom behavior and to suggest one potential approach for educators. Three sections will develop a perspective on these topics: the first will discuss the nature and causes of educational difficulties encountered by Native American college students, the second will discuss a communication competency

---

*Dr. Brooks Hill, Dr. H. Wayland Cummings, and Dr. Ralph Cooley all made significant contributions to the ideas presented in this paper.

approach to the problem, and the third will explore the ethical issues involved in such an approach.

EDUCATIONAL DIFFICULTIES AND COMMUNICATION BEHAVIOR

Despite the time and effort of many educators, the formal educational experience of Native American students remains negative. For example, a survey conducted at the University of Oklahoma (Carney, 1978, 1979) revealed a combined dropout rate for Indian men and women of 63%. The attrition rate for Indian women alone was 78%. The survey also reported lower grade-point averages for Native Americans than for their non-Indian counterparts; 37% accumulated a grade point average of less than 2.0 on a 4.0 scale. This situation is not limited to any particular institution, age, sex, or tribe. On a nationwide basis, Kleinfield and Kohout (1974) estimate that the college dropout rate may be as high as 93%.

Three very general explanations for this phenomenon exist. One blames the overall environment of educational institutions, and the second argues that the Native American cultural "attitude" is responsible. The third explanation suggests that it is the conflict between cultures which accounts for educational failure.

Critics of educational institutions (Carroll, 1978) emphasize that classroom requirements, dormitory facilities, and class offerings are diametrically opposed to Indian cultural needs and values. Indian students who attend colleges and universities are confronted with an environment that is bewildering and frustrating. The gulf between the expectations of the educational environment and those of the student's tribe seem insurmountable, thus creating an unbearable atmosphere which leads to academic failure.

The second perspective presumes that educational institutions are sound. This position argues that Indian students lack certain traits, skills, dispositions, or attitudes which are required for success. Native American students have been shown to be less motivated (Query et al., 1977), less intelligent (Church, 1976, 1977), and exhibit lower scores on various self-concept measures. These cultural differences presumably destine some Indian students to failure.

The third explanation argues that neither the institutional nor "person deficiency" perspectives offer complete explanations (Carroll, 1978; Kennan et al., 1979; Lujan et al., 1979). This position suggests that Native American classroom behavior may represent an intercultural communication strategy devised as a response to the environment (Dumont, 1972; Philips, 1972). Carroll (1978) makes a key observation in this regard by noting that potentially "good" students may be disruptive and may purposely perform at inferior levels just to maintain their "Indianness." Lujan et al. (1979) and Carroll (1978) raise the possibility that educational failure may be due in part to the institution and cultural differences, and in part to the conflicting value systems presented by the tribe and the educational institution.

In offering this hypothesis, Lujan et al. (1979) argue for two key points: First, the educational environment is one in which assimilation occurs; that is, where Indian students learn non-Indian culture. Second, college students, and Native Americans in particular, are seeking a sense of self-identity. For Indian students, however, personal identity is drawn from outside the university environment.

Indian students, thus, must deal with the dilemma that exists between their quest for self-identity and the acculturative aspects of education. The institution is distinctly non-Indian, while the orientation of the student is tribal. Thus, active participation in classroom activities implies assimilation into non-Indian culture; however, nonparticipation leads to educational failure, and thus a difficult paradox emerges.

The conflict between education and Indianness results in a particular intercultural communication strategy. Lujan et al., (1979) and Kennan et al. (1980) describe this response as a strategy of interactional avoidance. Its purpose is to maintain a balance between education and Indianness. By employing a communication strategy that limits interaction, Indian students assume that they are thwarting assimilation and protecting their Indianness. If the strategy functions well, this dilemma need not be directly confronted. Unfortunately, this strategy leads to educational failure in the majority of cases.

Current research interpreted along these lines suggests that there exists a complexity of communication behavior designed as an intercultural communication strategy. Lujan et al. (1979) and Kennan et al. (1980) have sought to describe relevant aspects of this strategy.

Lujan et al. (1979) conducted a 2-year longitudinal study of classroom interaction at the University of Oklahoma. The results of that study identified five categories of behavior that can be inductively correlated to educational failure. Those categories include complete withdrawal from the educational situation, nonparticipation in classroom discussions, refusal to respond to direct requests, time spent communicating, and eye contact. In all five cases the researchers suggested that the values for these categories were at variance with what would be judged as positive behavior by most teachers.

Kennan et al. (1980) described Native American classroom behavior by empirically analyzing communication interaction. The behavior of Indian college students was compared to Anglo-American behavior in small group settings. An interaction analysis based on a system that organizes communication acts into four categories (information exchange, problem solution-identification, negotiation, and behavior modification) was employed.

The results suggested that Native American college students exhibited significant differences in behavior from their Anglo-American counterparts. Those differences centered around how communication was established (negotiation), the means for regulating behavior (behavior modification), and how problems were solved (problem identification-solution).

In addition to the descriptions of behavior, both studies suggest that the repertoire of Native American classroom behavior involves much more than just a strategy of silence, and that the observed behavior appeared to be situational responses to the educational environment. Lujan et al. (1979) demonstrated that the same students who exhibited dysfunctional behavior in the classroom exhibited more positively evaluated behavior when in the tribal context. These findings seem to suggest that the difficulties faced by Indian students may be best attributed to a response based on contextual requirements rather than to any differentially inherent perceptions or skills.

Given the dilemma described in the foregoing pages, the teacher faced with coping with Native American students must obviously develop a functional response. The following section suggest directions and strategies for Native American education.

TEACHING INTERCULTURAL COMMUNICATION COMPETENCE

1. Coursework in Communication Skills

Given that intercultural communication is central to the problems raised, it seems obvious that an essential first step is to provide coursework in communication. This is not to suggest that Native Americans ought to be taught communication skills in the same way as non-Indian students. Rather, Indian students ought to be taught the competence required for effective intercultural communication in the educational context.

Although competence is difficult to identify from a research perspective, educators are capable of identifying and teaching some obvious correlates of classroom success. Thus, a variety of skills (public speaking, small group communication, interpersonal communication, etc.) may be taught as parts of a code system unique to non-Indian culture.

2. Competence Must be Taught as an Alternative Code

An approach that includes teaching various communication skills is not particularly new. A number of colleges and universities have established a wide variety of programs designed to improve the educational longevity of Indian students. Unfortunately, many of those efforts have attempted to *substitute* "appropriate" for "inappropriate" behavior. From such pursuits, Indian students come to fear losing their Indianness. Clearly, this is dysfunctional.

A more useful approach, then, is to teach alternative communication strategies as an alternative and *not* as a substitute. Further, Indian students must be constantly made aware that the use of such an alternative does not threaten self-identity or prevent them from operating successfully in the tribal context.

3. Approaching Cultural Pluralism

The traditional approach to Indian education has been that of assimilation. The purpose of legislation and the structure of schools has been to assimilate Indians into an Anglo-dominated culture, thus, making additional attention to the "Indian problem" unnecessary. Thus, typical Indian college-student performance is grounded in a well founded suspicion of the motives of educators. However, educators and students must come to agree that the United States is a pluralistic society; that the melting pot metaphor is a myth. Despite the pluralistic nature of our society, students must come to see that there exists the necessity for successful interaction. Thus, by learning and employing a new, more functional communication repertoire, students may come to realize that there is no necessity for assimilation and that they can successfully cope with the non-Indian educational environment.

4. A Comparison of Perspectives

An educational strategy founded on these recommendations must also include a careful comparison of current behavior with the suggested alternative in a low risk situation. It is essential that students be encouraged to articulate their concerns in a comfortable atmosphere. If the students feel targeted, the typical avoidance strategy will be elicited.

ETHICAL ISSUES

The educator thrust into the classroom with Native American students is rapidly made aware of an uncomfortable, if not ambiguous, ethical dilemma. To the degree that the student's behavior is modified to accomodate a more meaningful educational experience in the traditional style of public education, that student is effectively denied much of his or her own legitimate cultural experience. On the other hand, failure to provide appropriate avenues of intercultural success effectively denies students the benefits of traditional education. Put more simply, we are caught between the fundamental value of freedom of choice, which implies the right to a cultural experience un-fettered by manipulation, and the fact that no clear cut classroom strategy exists which completely avoids such manipulation. The strategies adopted for use in the classroom, *whatever* they are, will have a profound effect on the lives of Native American students.

Native American students themselves seem only partially aware of this dilemma. Their classroom behavior is symptomatic of a cultural conflict only partially realized but acutely felt. We cannot, then, allow students to self-select; that is, to make the choice for themselves. Asking one to choose between two options, neither of which is clearly understood, is equivalent to providing no option at all.

Past approaches to this problem almost uniformly have been directed toward assimilation. For all practical purposes, students have been isolated from their own cultural environment, either in boarding schools or in local schools where little effort has been made to cast the learning experience into the students' already achieved cultural perspective. In the Southwest United States, nearly any Native American over the age of 50 can recount stories of corporal punishment for such offenses as speaking their native language or "doing things in an Indian way." Such practices are not current, but the basic strategy of assimilation remains unchanged. Unfortunately, our colleges and universities are very slow in remedying this situation. Without intention, the college environment becomes a place where many Native Americans become unable to function within the framework of their own culture.

The creation of special programs or new areas of study for Native Americans tend to separate them from college life and, thus, risks providing them with an educational experience that is not useful in the everyday Anglo world.

Ethically, it is not for educators to choose for the student, but to bring students to the point of self-selection. An appropriate educational experience can make students more overtly aware of the choices they face and allow them to make informed choices.

REFERENCES

CARNEY, M.L. (1978). "Summary of Data Related to Attrition." (Studies conducted by the Office of Research for the University Community.) Norman, OK: University of Oklahoma.

CARNEY, M.L. (1979). "A Four Year Comparison of New Student Socioeconomic Background, Attitudes and Abilities: 1976-1979." Norman, OK: University of Oklahoma.

CARROLL, R.E. (1978). Academic performance and cultural marginality. *Journal of American Indian Education 18* (Oct.), 11-16.

CHURCH, A. (1976). Academic achievement, IQ, level of occupational plans, and ethnic stereotypes for Anglos and Navajos in a multi-ethnic high school. *Southern Journal of Educational Research 10*, 184-201.

CHURCH, A. (1977). Academic achievement, IQ, level of occupational plans and self-concepts for Anglo and Navajo school students. *Psychology 14* (Feb.), 24-40.

DUMONT, R. (1972). Learning English and how to be silent: Studies in Sioux and Cherokee classrooms. *In* C.B. Cazden, V.P. John, and D. Hymes (Eds.), "Functions of Language in the Classroom." New York: Teachers College Press.

KENNAN, W.R., CUMMINGS, H.W. and LUJAN, P.D. (1980). "A Descriptive Study of Intercultural Communication Between Native American and Anglo-American College Students." (Paper Presented at the Speech Communication Association Convention. New York.)

KLEINFIELD, J.S., and KOHOUT, K.L. (1974). Increasing the college success of Alaskan natives. *Journal of American Indian Education 13* (May), 27-31.

LUJAN, P., KENNAN, W.R., HILL, L.B., and LONG, L.W. (1979). "Communication Reticence of Native Americans in the Classroom: A Reconceptualization and Approach." Paper presented at the Speech Communication Association Convention. San Antonio, Texas.)

PHILIPS, S.U. (1972). Participant structures and communicative competence: Warm Springs children in community and classroom. *In* C.B. Cazden, V.P. John, and D. Hymes (Eds.), "Functions of Language in the Classroom." New York: Teachers College Press.

QUERY, J.M., QUERY, W.T., and SINGH, D. (1975). Independence training, need achievement and need affiliation. *International Journal of Psychology 10*, 255-268.

21

Teaching Interpersonal Communication Through
Novels, Plays, and Films

MARVIN D. JENSEN
University of Northern Iowa
Cedar Falls, Iowa 50614

William Faulkner (1968) believed that "art preserves life." He called for literature that explores the human spirit, a spirit that is "capable of compassion and sacrifice and endurance."

Such literature can be a means of applying and illustrating theories of interpersonal communication. This paper offers examples of theoretical concepts which can be illustrated through literature and popular film. The theories and applications cited are intended for college-level instruction.

Selection of novels, plays, and films for the study of human interaction should be based on two criteria: (a), These creative works should reflect reality, or "preserve life." The works must be honest, and contain sufficient depth to do justice to the subtleties and complexities of human beings (O'Connor, 1962, p.125). (b), These art forms should challenge comfortable assumptions and platitudes about human relationships—for there is a difference between normal behavior and natural behavior. Our task in studying human interaction is to search for whatever is natural, and such inquiry does not always produce expected or comfortable answers. James Karman (1981) recently commented on the challenging role that art and education should play. Reflecting on a student's complaint that his college courses had made him uncertain about life, Karman writes: "The title of a poem by Wallace Stevens came to mind: 'Poetry Is a Destructive Force.' So is all serious thought; so is all serious teaching."

The theories and interpretations suggested in this paper may be destructive to easy answers. Moreover, they do not provide new certainties—but attempt to raise questions which respect the complexity of human behavior. A collegiate course in interpersonal communication should do no less.

THEORIES OF ABRAHAM MASLOW APPLIED TO *A SEPARATE PEACE*

Abraham Maslow proposed five characteristics of the self-actualized person, based on his study of historical figures and his observation of exceptional students. He concluded that self-actualized persons have in common: (a), creativity; (b), spontaneity; (c), dedication to a vocation or task; (d), a clear perception of reality; and (e), a low degree of self-conflict (Gable, 1970, pp. 27-29). Phineas, in John Knowles' novel, *A Separate Peace* (1959), reflects these five characteristics. But the portrait is not uncomplicated, and the need to weigh carefully the motivations and behavior of Phineas allows a realistic application of Maslow's ideas. Although this novel is often studied in high school literature classes, it is a book that yields insight equivalent to the experience a reader brings to it. The novel appears to be based in part on John Knowles' own experiences at Exeter Academy during World War II; and it is significant that he waited 16 years to fully describe a remarkable young man he calls Phineas. Possibly only a mature and self-actualizing person can accurately perceive or describe another who is self-actualized.

As described by Knowles, Phineas meets the first three criteria of self-actualization. He is creative in his invention of games without losers. He is spontaneous in acknowledging affection to his friend, Gene—an act which Knowles calls nearly suicidal in the atmosphere of a prep school. He is dedicated to any task he undertakes—from athletic achievement to leadership in school activities.

The last two criteria are not so obviously illustrated by Phineas. His apparent denial that Gene shook the tree and caused his crippling accident may be taken as evidence that Phineas is unwilling or unable to admit reality. But possibly the self-actualized person is one who asks more difficult questions and achieves a clearer (albeit more complicated) perception of reality. The other boys at the academy, including Gene, are preoccupied with the question "what happened"—and are eager to assess blame. Phineas asks the far more difficult question: "why did it happen?" The answer he reaches is tempered by emotional and physical suffering, and cannot be dismissed as a superficial denial of reality. Phineas concludes that there are sometimes blind impulses in life, which (despite tragic consequences) are neither planned nor malicious. This insight may allow the self-actualized person to transcend revenge and absolve another from guilt—not out of foolish innocence, but out of wisdom about human imperfection. Maslow's last criterion (a low degree of self-conflict) also appears, at first reading, to be contradicted by Phineas. His efforts to enter the army in spite of his shattered leg, and his apparent desire to conform to war-time sentiments, seem in sharp conflict with his usual independent thinking and rejection of competition. Yet, from the title of the book to its closing lines, *A Separate Peace* may be seen as describing an underlying consistency in attitude and behavior. Had he entered the war, Phineas would probably have brought his blitzball game to the front lines—a game in which the players keep changing sides. Or he might have brought to the war zone the American Indian tradition of "counting coup"—approaching an enemy close enough to kill him, only to touch his shoulder and turn away. Or, more literally, he might have been among the World War II infantry who went to the front lines, but declined to fire their guns. This would be consistent with his behavior at the academy, when he breaks a swimming record without announcing it, and charms the faculty while skipping classes and escaping to the beach. A self-actualized person knows the rules, and can play by them—but may choose not to. The separate peace known by a self-actualized person may include the recognition that our greatest enemies are competition, suspicion, and guilt—and freedom from them is achieved in the mind, not on the battlefield.

THEORIES OF CHARLES HAMPDEN-TURNER AND VIKTOR FRANKL APPLIED TO *MY MORTAL ENEMY*

A second author whose novels and short fiction offer particular insights into human behavior is Willa Cather. Her writings can be used to apply the theories of Charles Hampden-Turner and Viktor Frankl.

Charles Hampden-Turner has criticized the approach of traditional social scientists, who reach conclusions about human behavior based on averages and statistical norms. He believes this approach is common because it is relatively easy. Like the man searching for his lost wallet only where the light is best, social scientists often reach conclusions based primarily on the typical, majority behavior which is most visible. But there is a difference between typical behavior and natural behavior—and Hampden-Turner (1970, pp. 9-14) urges the study of the exceptional individual who innovates, deviates, dreams, creates, and resists.

Viktor Frankl witnessed exceptional human behavior during his years in Nazi concentration camps and believes that freedom and meaning are found through individual responses to life's conditions. Frankl (1963) offers a renewed importance to the word "responsibility" by defining it as "the ability to respond." Response-ability, even when facing the worst conditions and most oppressive constraints, is Frankl's answer to the behaviorist vision of conditioning, programming, stimulus-response, and behavior modification.

Willa Cather came to similar conclusions from an artist's view as she explored and honored the exceptional person. She wrote from her own experiences and observations, and the reality of her characterizations is unmistakable. Through her short stories and novels, she spoke of the heroic (but never idealized) person—often in battle with surrounding conditions or his/her own lesser self. In the preface to Cather's novel *My Mortal Enemy*, Marcus Klein (1961, p. vi) writes of her human portrayals: "all struggled toward an image of poised and indisputable greatness, by which everything that cluttered, everything that was tawdry and cheap and small and restricting, would be subdued." In *My Mortal Enemy* (Cather, 1926), Myra Henshawe is a flawed and eccentric woman—but she twice rises above tawdriness. As a young woman, she rejects the restrictions of her great-uncle's fortune in favor of her own choice of husband. As an old woman, she rejects the restrictions of poverty by spending her last coins on a Mass to honor the actress Helena Modjeska, and then secures a taxi to take her from her tenement room to see the ocean and the dawn before she dies. Myra Henshawe reaches for her natural and best self in these acts, and perhaps teaches us again that the "hero is just an ordinary person who, for a moment, isn't."

THEORIES OF R. D. LAING APPLIED TO *EQUUS*

R. D. Laing is a Scottish psychiatrist whose views have become known as anti-psychiatry. His writing and its applications are particularly relevant to lay students, because he contends that troubled behavior and breakdowns in relationships are too often turned over to "experts." Laing believes this leads to diagnosis, labeling, and treatment—when the real need is often for attention and affection, which are the province of all human beings, not just experts. Laing argues that the disorder labeled "schizophrenia" is not a breakdown, but a breakthrough of the hidden inner self which has become so separated from the outer self that it abruptly closes like a screen door that is opened too wide. A person experiencing such a breakthrough, according to Laing, needs support and acceptance—not treatment which is designed to restore the former outer self (a re-opening of the screen door). Laing also believes that human beings are capable of dealing with any reality, but not with hypocrisy. He suggests, as many others have, that unusual behavior does not mean a person is mad; possibly it is the world that is mad (Gordon, 1971).

Among the books which illustrate Laing's ideas are *Two Accounts of a Journey Through Madness* (Bernes and Berke, 1971) (an autobiographical record of a recovered "schizophrenic" who lived in a community arrangement with Laing and others), and *I Never Promised You a Rose Garden* (Green, 1964) (a fictionalized autobiography of a young woman who chooses reality over fantasy with the support of a psychiatrist who is modeled on one of Laing's colleagues).

An additional work of fiction which allows exploration of Laing's thinking is the play *Equus* by Peter Shaffer (1974). The play describes the relationship between Martin Dysart (a psychiatrist) and Alan Strang (who is institutionalized after blinding six horses). It becomes clear that Alan's act was a break-through of frustration and anger in the face of religious obsession by his mother and sexual hypocrisy by his father. The lack of open family relations leads Alan to focus his affection on horses, but he eventually transfers to them his rage at being watched and judged. Alan Strang's troubles are revealed not only by his violent act, but by his inability to respond to the affection of a young woman he cares for. Shaffer implies in his play that the psychiatrist should have helped Alan by offering him understanding rather than a "cure." But Martin Dysart's own inadequacies cause him to be threatened by the intensity of Alan's misdirected passion. He stands accused by Alan's words: "At least I galloped! When did you?" (Shaffer, 1974, p. 94). Near the end of the play, this fictional psychiatrist acknowledges the flaw of psychiatry which Laing implies: "Passion, you see, can be destroyed by a doctor. It cannot be created" (Shaffer, 1974, p.124). The blurring of who is mad and who is sane, who normal and who abnormal, is complete when Dysart gives up the pursuit of a supportive interpersonal relationship with the boy and chooses treatment instead. Dysart's words in the last scene echo Laing's criticism of psychiatry. Dysart says: ". . . I'll set him on a nice mini-scooter and send him puttering off into the Normal world where animals are treated properly: made extinct, or put into servitude, or tethered all their lives in dim light. . . . You won't gallop any more, Alan. Horses will be quite safe" (Shaffer, 1974, p. 125).

If *I Never Promised You a Rose Garden* were studied along with *Equus*, the reader/student would perceive the contast between a gradual progression into a healthy freeing relationship, and a regression into conditioning and treatment.

THEORIES OF THOMAS SZASZ APPLIED TO *WHOSE LIFE IS IT ANYWAY?*

Thomas Szasz is a professor of psychiatry whose views also challenge the traditional premises of his profession. He believes that the imposition of laws against victimless "crimes," and the labeling of unusual behavior as "sickness," creates oppression of the individual (Szasz, 1974, 1980). Like Laing, Szasz recognizes that some people are genuinely troubled and self-destructive, but suggests that acceptance, support, and understanding are more helpful than the imposition of norms. Both Laing and Szasz carry to a logical extension Carl Rogers' (1961, p. 63) philosophy of "unconditional positive regard." Szasz argues that no behavior should be repressed by either legal or medical means as long as such behavior is not destructive to another person. But his rejection of legal and medical restraints does not mean the withholding of personal concern and influence.

Among the most controversial of Szasz's ideas is his contention that suicide is an individual's right. The implications of this idea are explored in Brian Clark's play *Whose Life Is It Anyway?* (1974). This play explores the dilemma of a mature, intelligent man who is paralyzed when his spinal column is injured in an automobile accident. Because there is no hope of recovery and he does not want to live in that condition, Ken Harrison requests that the life support systems be disconnected. In response to this request, the doctor diagnoses his patient as depressed and prescribes tranquilizers. Mr. Harrison argues that it is rational and even healthy to be depressed under such circumstances, and his need is not for tranquilizers—but the right to a dignified death. Eventually, the patient seeks legal aid (no easy task, since all resistance to treatment is considered a symptom of depression requiring more treatment). Although this play is partially about medical ethics and legal rights, it is primarily about intrapersonal and interpersonal communication. It shows the difficulty of responding to a double bind situation. It illustrates the difference between medical personnel who *take care of* a patient, and those who *care for* a fellow human being. Finally, it confronts the reader or viewer with the reality that a decision to die can be both rational and natural—and that acceptance of it has a place in human relationships.

THEORIES OF ALBERT ELLIS APPLIED TO *ORDINARY PEOPLE*

Like novels and plays, films can be a means of studying interpersonal communication. The film *Ordinary People* succeeds in depicting reality. The novel by Judith Guest (1976) captures the breakdown of communication within a family, and the film retains the authenticity of her novel—while providing additional visual and nonverbal nuances which increase our identification with the characters.

The film can serve as a vehicle for studying the rational-emotive process described by Albert Ellis (1973). Ellis disagrees with B. F. Skinner's (1957) stimulus-response description of human behavior. Instead, he suggests a three-step process: the activating experience, beliefs about the experience, and response. If the beliefs are irrational, the response is going to be destructive—but this unhealthy response is a result of the belief, not the original activating experience. Ellis believes that this A-B-C path can be re-channeled into an A-D-E progression in which a person makes a rational dispute of the situation, which can lead to a healthy response. In *Ordinary People*, the activating experience is the accidental death of the older son. Mother, father, and younger son all hold the irrational belief that someone is to blame. This shared belief leads to serious breakdowns in family relationships, although the unhealthy responses differ with each family member. The mother retreats into cold bitterness, the father suffers increasing frustration and depression, and the younger son Conrad is plagued by guilt because he survived the boating accident that killed his brother. Ellis's analysis can be applied not only to understand their attitudes, but to explore alternative attitudes. If each of the three could have rationally questioned the situation, each could have seen that it was a tragic accident for which no one was to blame. The resulting responses could have been healthier, shared expressions of grief and loss.

CONCLUSION

Carefully chosen literature and film can help us to better understand and appreciate the intricacies of human communication. The best writers and film makers accept Faulkner's (1968, p. 127) challenge to go beyond the "ephemeral" and rediscover "love and honor and pity and pride and compassion and sacrifice." Theoretical analysis and creative insight are parallel paths to truth. Students of interpersonal communication are well served when theories are applied, and when those applications authentically "preserve life."

REFERENCES

BARNES M., and BERKE, J. (1971). "Two Accounts of a Journey Through Madness." New York: Harcourt Brace Jovanovich.

CATHER, W. (1926). "My Mortal Enemy." New York: Alfred A. Knopf.

CLARK, B. (1974). "Whose Life Is It Anyway?" Chicago, IL: The Dramatic Publishing Company.

ELLIS, A. (1973). "Humanistic Psychotherapy: The Rational-Emotive Approach." New York: Julian Press.

FAULKNER, W. (1968). On accepting the Nobel prize for literature. In B. Aly and L. F. Aly (Eds.), "American Short Speeches." New York: Macmillan.

FRANKL, V. (1963). "Man's Search for Meaning: An Introduction to Logotherapy." New York: Washington Square Press.

GABLE, F. (1970). "The Third Force." New York: Pocket Books.

GORDON, J. S. (1971). Who is mad? Who is sane? *Atlantic* (Jan.), 50-66.

GREEN, H. (1964). "I Never Promised You a Rose Garden." New York: Holt, Rinehart and Winston.

GUEST, J. (1976). "Ordinary People." New York: Viking.

HAMPDEN-TURNER, C. (1970). "Radical Man." Garden City, NY: Anchor Books.

KARMAN J. (1981). If we try to blunt the edge of a great idea to "protect" our students, education suffers. *Chronicle of Higher Education* (Mar. 23), 64.

KLEIN, M. (1961). Introduction. In W. Cather, "My Mortal Enemy." New York: Vintage Books.

KNOWLES, J. (1959). "A Separate Peace." New York: Bantam Books.

O'CONNOR, F. (1962). "Mystery and Manners." New York: Farrar, Straus and Giroux.

ROGERS, C. R. (1961). "On Becoming a Person." Boston: Houghton Mifflin.

SHAFFER P. (1974). "Equus." New York: Avon Books.

SKINNER, B. F. (1957). "Verbal Behavior." Englewood Cliffs, NJ: Prentice-Hall.

SZASZ, T. (1974). Our despotic laws destroy the right to self-control. *Psychology Today* 8 (No. 7), 19-29, 127.

SZASZ, T. (1980). Therapeutic tyranny. *OMNI* 2 (No. 6), 43.

Author Index

Italic page numbers indicate bibliographic citations.

Subject Index